Lone Gunman

Phil La Duke

Rewriting the Handbook On Workplace Violence Prevention

ISBN: 978-1-945853-15-9

Printed by Marriah Publishing

New Jersey, the United States of America

INSERT DATE PUBLICATION

Testimonials

"I took time out of a busy schedule to read Phil LaDuke's latest book -- *Lone Gunman: Rewriting the Rulebook on Workplace Violence* because I knew it was important. Women are very often the victims of violence and the workplace is no exception. I know the problem; what I appreciated as a small business owner were the ideas about how to identify people and scenarios that could become problematic. A good read."

-Paula Talarico, Attorney and Women's Rights Activist

"**Chris Rock once said:** *"You can only offend me if you mean something to me"*. Phil's writing doesn't pull punches and may be a bit like someone swinging a bag of broken glass in a crowded room but if his words cut deep and gouge a lot of nerves it's only because he has the insight and courage to articulate what many of us are thinking and, for the rest, still struggling with weird feelings, he puts his gnarly finger right on it. People love him because he has empathy and vents on their behalf, people hate him because he has figured them out, exposed them, challenged their worldview and sent their cognitive dissonance into meltdown. Either way, Phil's writing means something to everyone. He has inspired and completely changed the trajectory and style of my own writing. In the words of another safety literary legend and fellow Phil Fan, the late George Robotham: *"It would be a boring world if everybody agreed with me"*.

—Dave Collins, Creator, Editor, and Publisher https://safetyrisk.net/

"Phil's passion comes through in virtually everything he writes. He is an outspoken advocate for employee engagement and respect for workers"

—Dr. Paul Marciano, Best selling author of Carrots and Sticks Don't Work: Build a Culture of Employee Engagement with the Principles of Respect and Super Teams:Using the Principles of Respect to Unleash Explosive Business Performance

"Phil La Duke is an original. After Phil they broke the mold. Certainly his thoughts and ideas on workplace safety and health fit no mold. Phil is no safety drone. His writing is provocative, sometime blunt, sometimes insulting, sometimes raw. His is an outsider's take, almost an outlaw's take, on what is good, bad and ugly about current workplace safety thinking and practices. It's a perspective you won't find anywhere else."

—Dave Johnson, Editor. ISHN magazine

"Phil La Duke has devoted his career to industrial safety. He knows the importance of doing an unglamorous job well and what goes terribly wrong when people don't. He is angry about all the right things.

—Peter Page, contributed content editor Entrepreneur magazine

Phil LaDuke truly shatters the decades-old mindsets of safety professionals that have mired the profession in ideological adherence to accident safety practices, while stifling the introduction of innovative approaches. Provocative as Phil is, he brings a refreshing counterbalance to the safety conversation and makes us think. Indeed, Phil is the "Dirty Jobs Mike Rowe" of the safety profession.

—James E. Leemann, Ph.D.

Introduction

Those of you who know me know I don't pull punches, which I acknowledge is a strange expression to use in the first line of a book about preventing workplace violence, but you should know this going in. I am not ones to mince words and this subject matter is something very important to me.

I personally have been deeply affected because a factory at which I was previously employed as a consultant was the scene of a single shooter workplace violence event and a man who I knew was killed. Most days I don't even want to GO to work (even though for the most part I love my job) let alone die there. In the history of mankind, I seriously and whole heartedly believe that given the choice of a place to die, no one EVER chose to die at work.

I think of him, a man who was a Union Rep who had no part in the circumstances that led to this violence, lying on a dirty factory floor his last moments on this Earth, the last moments of his life spent bewildered, wondering what just happened to him as his lifeblood pooled and mingled with the ever-present machine oil and grime on the floor. What stunned me was how easy it was for an armed man to enter a guarded facility, methodically and unchallenged seek out his estranged girlfriend and gun her down and two others just for good measure.

This is real to me and it should be real to you. This isn't something that happens to other people at other facilities. And in this climate of hate and violence, where bombastic blowhards preach violence and hate it's likely that these events will increase.

I started this book at the request of my publisher long before the recent rash of mass shootings. I am a conniving, opportunistic little troll, but even I wouldn't sink so low as to capitalize on the epidemic of carnage that has plagued us recently.

The 24-news cycle brings tragedy into our homes daily, and it's easy to believe that workplace violence is at an epidemic level, but that is not the case. According to the US Bureau of Labor Statistics, workplace homicides rose by only 2% in 2015 while shootings overall had risen 15%. Even so, while gun rights advocates and opponents alike can argue over the extent of the problem, that is not the intent of this book. I grew up on a farm and around firearms and while I do not own firearms, I firmly believe that the mere availability of guns is not the root cause of this problem. The availability of baseball bats is far more common and yet we seldom see a person grabbing a bat and heading to the workplace to bash some skulls (although some of us may feel like it from time to time).

This is not a subject about which I should be glib, but most people seem to forget about the extent of the problem so perhaps an emotional kick in the gut is what we need to take this issue more seriously. And it's certainly worth noting that while we all might feel the urge to choke out our bosses or a coworker from time to time—most of us don't and won't—but to be on the safe side, if I put food in the refrigerator (even if I don't put my name on it) if you have any sense of self-preservation you won't eat it. And frankly, why would you? You know it isn't yours. Fortunately, I go out to lunch, but it's little things like this that can fester into real conflicts and add mental illness and alcohol into that mix and you may just get a violent outburst. Seriously though, what kind of person eats someone else's lunch and thinks that it's okay?

You may have noticed that I use humor a lot in my writing and some people are put off by it. This book is no exception. I find that making a joke before or after making a serious point tends to help people retain the serious points. And this book is about a serious issue, so serious in fact, that were I not to lighten it up once and again it could become so depressing that I would struggle to write it and you would struggle to read it. If you can't handle that, might I suggest a nice coloring book or perhaps *The Little House in The Big Woods* it's not funny and won't help you survive a workplace shooting but then there's always a trade-off.

The resulting tome would be good for killing the occasional centipede or for use as a doorstop but would be useless for its intended purpose, which is, to act as a guide and a handbook to any and all of you who want to protect your workplace from single shooter events. So I won't apologize to you if my use of humor offends your delicate sensibilities or neurotic compulsion to be politically correct because the points that you remember through the lens of your righteous indignation might just save multiple lives.

Acknowledgments

This book could not be possible with the love and support of my family and friends, my publisher and public relations manager ...oh hell I can't type this drivel. Let's give credit where credit is due. This book could not be possible without the manufacturers of Diet Dr. Pepper whose product is directly responsible for my ability to write at the speed of light, the Labatt brewing company, makers of Labatt's Blue, the owners of Party Stop Liquor Store and Timothy O'Malley's bar that keep me drunk enough to come down from the caffeine coursing through my veins. And of course, the manufacturers of clonazepam and all the other drugs that comprise the cocktail that keeps me alive.

Of course, I would be remiss if I didn't acknowledge the menagerie of maniacs that have crossed my path, and the sickening pussbag-bullies who made it so easy to understand— while neither condoning or accepting—how someone could go off the rails and shoot up a workplace.

My heartfelt sympathy goes out to the victims of workplace violence and all those who mourn them. This book is for you, may it save lives where your life could have been.

Chapter 1: Background & History

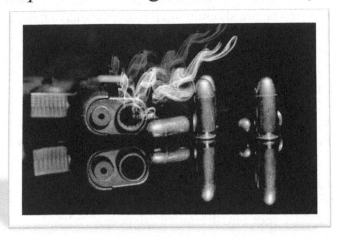

Before we can continue, we need to clarify some unsettling and misleading information and dispel some very, and perhaps deliberately, misleading beliefs.

Claim: Workplace Violence and Mass Shootings are the same.

Fact: Mass shootings, that is, a shooting where a lone gunman or small group of gunmen attack a crowd of people. Mass shooters may claim to be guided by some misguided ideology or bigotry but in my opinion, they just want to kill people. They have been with us since the dawn of time. What makes them tick? Frankly, I don't care I'll leave that to the sociologists and criminologist to suss out. The people gunned downed by these human pustules not knowing their motivation are just as dead as the ones who understand them completely. They are mad dog killers and should be treated like Old Yeller. Don't read this book looking for insights into the mind of mass shooters; you won't find any. This book is designed to guide you in protecting workers from single shooter events in the workplace.

Mass shooters don't really care who they shoot, yes, they may want to shoot Jews, or African Americans, or Liberals, or whomever, but IF they have a specific group, they are targeting they typically aren't targeting specific individuals, whereas lone gunmen who are shooting up a workplace have a specific target or targets in mind. Occasional an innocent bystander may be harmed, but to the shooter that is just collateral damage and not the result of the shooter wanting to increase his body count. Note: I spoke to law enforcement agents and I can tell you with some certainty that there is great confusion as to how to handle workplace murderers and mass shooters, and the tendency to view these two types as the same is very dangerous and chilling.

Claim: Workplace violence is all the same.

Fact: A relatively small amount of people who died of a homicide at work were true victims of workplace violence as defined in the scope of this work. Policemen, for example, certainly are shot in the course of their workdays, and while unacceptable the nature of the work makes them foreseeable targets.

Claim: Workplace violence is decreasing.

Fact: While the number of workplace violence incidents has been steadily decreasing since 1994 this number is misleading. In fact, in his article *6 Things to Know about Mass Shootings in America: As We Mourn The Victims Of Another Mass Shooting, A Criminologist Takes On Misconceptions About Gun Violence* published in 2016 in Scientific American, Frederic Lemieux said, "A recent study published by the Harvard Injury Control Research Center shows that the frequency of mass shooting is increasing over time. The researchers measured the increase by calculating the time between the occurrence of mass shootings. According to the research, the days separating mass shooting occurrence went from on average 200 days during the period of 1983 to 2011 to 64 days since 2011.

16

What is most alarming with mass shootings is the fact that this increasing trend is moving in the opposite direction of overall intentional homicide rates in the US, which decreased by almost 50% since 1993 and in Europe where intentional homicides decreased by 40% between 2003 and 2013.[1]

Claim: It is better to have your employees armed than unarmed.

Fact: The chances of your workplace being the scene of a deadly attack are extremely remote (remember you and your employees are over 10 times more likely to be killed in an automobile accident during your/their daily commute than they are to be murdered at work). This particular issue is hotly contested. Pro-armed workplace point to the statistic that typically where gun violence has been thwarted it has been in the hands of the first "friendly responder". As one police officer told me, "If you have 7 people sitting in cubes and a gunman comes in they will likely shoot him dead and there will be a much lower body count. When I questioned his assertion, he made some qualifications: IF the armed employees are well trained, and IF the employees are completely comfortable with ~~firearm~~, and IF they are excellent shots, and IF they employee ~~...~~ and IF the employee has the ability to take a ~~...~~tion where that is necessary---and ~~...~~forcement.

~~...~~ment receives is
~~...~~ y certainty what
~~...~~. Almost to prove
~~...~~al of the teachers

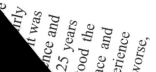

our children but trust them with firearms they don't use, furthermore, we don't pay for their teaching supplies but we're gonna buy them glocks? I doubt it.

Claim: Most people cannot hit anything with a pistol and you are better off running because most people can't even hit a moving target.

Fact: Most people aren't mass shooters or workplace murderers. For my part, I am extremely accurate with a pistol and don't own one and haven't fired one in over five years. I also have numerous friends and family who hunt and if they don't come home with a dead deer it's because they didn't see one NOT because they can't hit a moving target. Also, the mass shooter/workplace murderer has planned the assault (and as far as I know nobody that I know are planning such an endeavor) and fantasized about the assault. What would make people think that they are less capable of hitting a moving target than the many target shooters, skeet shooters, or hunters out there (of which there are hundreds of thousands who are law abiding citizens)?

Claim: You are more likely to be murdered at work than outside of work

Fact: The incidence of workplace homicides is much lower than homicides that take place elsewhere.

Clearly, this issue is important because 46% of workplace fatalities are homicides and they are, in fact, the leading cause of workplace fatalities, and while workplace injuries have fallen over time, workplace fatalities continue to trend fairly flat. So while the problem may not seem nearly as bad as 25 years ago, for the many victims of workplace violence those who mourn them, there is still a problem, an

What is most alarming with mass shootings is the fact that this increasing trend is moving in the opposite direction of overall intentional homicide rates in the US, which decreased by almost 50% since 1993 and in Europe where intentional homicides decreased by 40% between 2003 and 2013.[1]

Claim: It is better to have your employees armed than unarmed.

Fact: The chances of your workplace being the scene of a deadly attack are extremely remote (remember you and your employees are over 10 times more likely to be killed in an automobile accident during your/their daily commute than they are to be murdered at work). This particular issue is hotly contested. Pro-armed workplace point to the statistic that typically where gun violence has been thwarted it has been in the hands of the first "friendly responder". As one police officer told me, "If you have 7 people sitting in cubes and a gunman comes in they will likely shoot him dead and there will be a much lower body count. When I questioned his assertion, he made some qualifications: IF the armed employees are well trained, and IF the employees are completely comfortable with a firearm, and IF they are excellent shots, and IF they employee doesn't panic, and IF the employee has the ability to take a human life where in a situation where that is necessary---and that is not an easy to do even for law enforcement.

He also said that the training that (law enforcement receives is so contradictory that it is difficult to say with any certainty what the best thing to do in this situation would be. Almost to prove his point, in a recent school shooting several of the teachers were armed but did not pull their firearms for fear of being mistaken for the shooter. We don't trust our teachers to spank

---

[1]   *Source:* https://www.scientificamerican.com/article/6-things-to-know-about-mass-shootings-in-america/

our children but trust them with firearms they don't use, furthermore, we don't pay for their teaching supplies but we're gonna buy them glocks? I doubt it.

Claim: Most people cannot hit anything with a pistol and you are better off running because most people can't even hit a moving target.

Fact: Most people aren't mass shooters or workplace murderers. For my part, I am extremely accurate with a pistol and don't own one and haven't fired one in over five years. I also have numerous friends and family who hunt and if they don't come home with a dead deer it's because they didn't see one NOT because they can't hit a moving target. Also, the mass shooter/workplace murderer has planned the assault (and as far as I know nobody that I know are planning such an endeavor) and fantasized about the assault. What would make people think that they are less capable of hitting a moving target than the many target shooters, skeet shooters, or hunters out there (of which there are hundreds of thousands who are law abiding citizens)?

Claim: You are more likely to be murdered at work than outside of work

Fact: The incidence of workplace homicides is much lower than homicides that take place elsewhere.

Clearly, this issue is important because 46% of workplace fatalities are homicides and they are, in fact, the leading cause of workplace fatalities, and while workplace injuries have fallen over time, workplace fatalities continue to trend fairly flat. So while the problem may not seem nearly as bad as it was 25 years ago, for the many victims of workplace violence and those who mourn them, there is still a problem, and 25 years means that nearly an entire generation who understood the dangers of workplace violence have left the workplace and been replaced by workers who have little or no experience dealing with workplace homicides. To make matters worse, worker violence related to work but that is perpetrated outside of work is not calculated in these statistics. Instances where a lone gunman stalked workers and either shot and killed them as soon as they left the premises, or waited until they reached a nearby watering hole where he left them dead in the parking lot don't get tallied in the workplace homicide statistics. It's a problem and my job in writing this book is to help you in some small measure, to keep this from happening on your watch. [2]

When we talk about workplace violence, we could conceivably be talking about anything from a shoving match between to coworkers to a cold-blooded killer moving methodically through the workplace killing all he encounters. You might have noticed that I used the pronoun "he" in this sentence; that's deliberate. Perpetrators of workplace violence in the workplace are disproportionately male and 85% of these crimes are committed using a firearm although stabbings and beatings are not unheard of—you just have a better chance of surviving these types of attacks.

I won't drone on and on about how these are correlations and not cause and effect. And drawing conclusions based on these correlations can be dangerous. In his book *Blunders: Why Smart People Make Bad Decisions,* Zachery Shore coins the term, "Causefusion" to describe the confusion that so often leads to the mistaken belief that correlation equals cause and effect. Shore cites historical events where people, blinded by causefusion make devastating errors because of this cognitive blind. One of my favorite examples, come not from Shore, but from a friend of mine, is the almost perfect correlation between shark attacks and people eating ice cream.

It is a fact that shark attacks increase sharply about the same time that people increase their ice cream intake. The correlation is almost perfect. Does this mean that eating ice

---

[2] *It is important to remember that many of these previous workplace murders were really mass shooting in the workplace and disproportionately at postal facilities, which we will discuss in a later chapter.*

cream drives sharks to hunt that deliciously well-marbled human flesh? No, but it happens that a third element (and maybe more) is present—when it is warm more people swim in the ocean and more people eat ice cream. A similar correlation exists between autism and vaccinations.

Here again, the correlation can be misleading because of the of another fact: children tend to be vaccinated at about the same age or slightly exhibit signs of autism. Does a correlation exist? Absolutely. Does this mean that cause and effect exist in these cases? Most Doctors and researchers would give a resounding "no", and yet the belief still persists.

Some other correlations worth considering are the number of women who are veterans of wars, the number of women suffering PTSD, etc. One could postulate that because the opportunities and life experiences of women in 2018 that are dramatically different than they were in 1994 would likely have caused an uptick in women committing workplace homicides, fortunately, no such uptick exists.

The point is that no matter how logical we might find a correlation we can't extrapolate from that data and conclude, for example, that because there are more women serving in the military (and therefore more comfortable with guns) that more women will commit gun violence against a co-worker; it is a belief unsupported by facts. So, let's stick to what we know to be true and leave the creation of Urban Legends to hysterical social media nitwits.

Violence and Its Relationship to Occupation

It's not just your gender that makes you more or less likely to be murdered in the workplace. Some occupations are, by the very nature of the job, more prone to death by homicide than others—policemen, taxi drivers, and retail sales clerks all face a much higher risk of being murdered on the job than most occupations.

It makes sense that policemen would be victims of workplace violence; it is endemic to their jobs and even though it is a terrible thing for a law enforcement agent to die on the job it is certainly more expected than a drywall installer being gunned down. The very nature of their jobs puts them at risk, however, 2017 saw a 50-year low in police killed in the line of duty and of the 128 officers listed as killed in the line of duty only 44 were actually shot and killed. In fact, the single leading causes of the death of a police officer, on-the-job deaths are single vehicle accidents. [3]

---

[3] *Source: http://www.nleomf.org/assets/pdfs/reports/fatality-reports/2017/2017-End-of-Year-Officer-Fatalities-Report_FINAL.pdf*

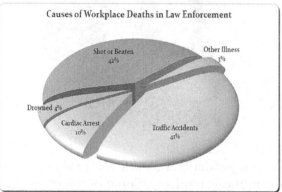

Causes of Workplace Deaths in Law Enforcement

Shot or Beaten 42%

Other Illness 3%

Drowned 4%

Cardiac Arrest 10%

Traffic Accidents 41%

While certainly tragic, this is a remarkably low number considering the sheer number of police interacting with citizens in an emotionally heightened state, or intentionally seeking harm to police officers. It is important to note that while police deaths in traffic accidents fell 13% from the previous year (2016 versus 2017) police who were shot to death has fallen 33% in fact if we adjust the chart to show police who have been killed as a result of deliberate violence committed upon them our chart shifts dramatically.

I got some push back from a policeman friend of mine when I cited the statistics that attacks on police and subsequent police deaths were inaccurate. A friend of his, went on to say that in many cases the person in the police department who is charged with reporting such statistics often downplay or even out-and-out deliberately lie to make the statistics look better than they actually are. For my part, I am not prepared to call police officers liars. For law enforcement agents wishing to refute the assertion that many of you routinely lie, please contact me and I will gladly provide you his name and address; maybe you can convince him of the lack of veracity of the statements made by police where I cannot.

Death by Homicide vs. Other Causes

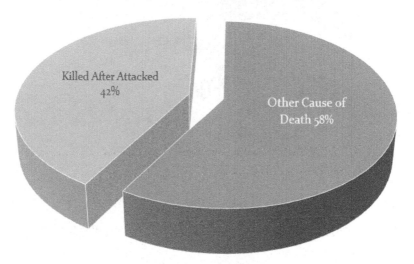

Aside from police, 500 people died in workplace homicides in 2018 and of that 152 were killed during robberies. Again, not to diminish the losses faced by those who have lost loved ones to robberies it skews the data and forces us to lose perspective.

Preventing robbery homicides is quite different than preventing workplace violence. To prevent workplace robbery homicides, we would have to focus on preventing robberies and while this is certainly something worth doing, that lies with the purview of law enforcement and governments. Unless you, yourself are an armed robber, there isn't much you can do to prevent robbery homicides.

Furthermore, we can never be quite certain why someone was killed during a robbery, homicides during a robbery represent a very small percentage or overall robberies and we don't know whether the victim recognized the assailant, panicked and caused the assailant to react, or if the assailant was just an asshat that wanted to kill someone.

Top 5 Robbery-Related Deaths by Occupation

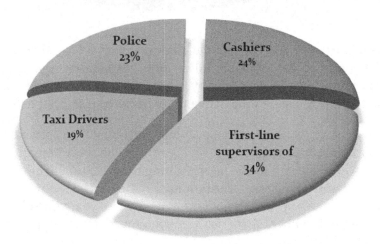

According to estimates by the National Safety Council, while traffic fatalities were down in 2017 they estimate that over 40,000 people died in US highway accidents. In other words, you are approximately 115 times more likely to die commuting to or from work than you are dying by being murdered at work. For me these statistics don't tell the whole story, a friend of mine's daughter, a single mother, was murdered execution style at midday, on camera, as she worked at one of those payday loan businesses. Robbery was the official motive and the case remains unsolved and the killer presumably at large,

It's worth noting that 23.4% of robbery fatalities are police officers so this is where some of the confusion may be coming from—these deaths are in effect being double counted: police killed in a robbery are a subset of those who are killed in the line of duty as the result of a shooting in any circumstance. In either case, it's irrelevant to the goal of this book, but if it shuts some slobbering critic up before the fact it's worth the ink.

It's also worth remembering, that lone shooter events in the workplace are not the same as school shootings or other mass shootings by unstable individuals attacking soft targets—these are mass murders and they are as different from workplace violence as they are from serial killings.

Mass murderers often will espouse a hatred of this group or that, but the reality is that these asshats just like killing, as do serial killers. These individuals fit an altogether different psychological profile, and while this is certainly an issue worth discussing, here again, that is beyond the scope of this work. Perpetrators of workplace violence tend to have very specific, albeit twisted motives and it's typically one of two:

1) a domestic squabble gone off the rails, or

2) a real or imagined grievance against the company.

In any event, despite a single shooter event in the workplace is a problem that somehow people now seem to believe that single shooter events are no longer a problem and that we can file it away as a remnant of a bygone age: it isn't.

I have two tragic experiences with domestic squabbles gone horribly awry, although neither happened in the workplace. The first happened to a close friend of mine from high school who was butchered by her estranged husband who stabbed her so many times that he literally broke the knife and then went back into the kitchen to get a fresh one to complete the job. He was convicted of second-degree murder and sentenced to 41/2 years in prison.

I want everyone reading this to think about this: This man has a job. This man likely has a wife or girlfriend. And this man now has already murdered one woman which demonstrates that he is physically and psychologically capable of doing it again, whether at home or in the workplace. Now I want you to ask yourselves, "how much do you know about who you or your daughter is dating?"

I'm not nearly as close to the second event as to the first, but in this case the angry (it's unclear if he was estranged or they were just fighting) boyfriend of a young woman who lived in my tiny home town (a fetid little village that makes Hooterville look like the Algonquin Round Table) went to her home, forced his way in and brutally murdered her parents. He then rigged the door with an explosive booby trap and waited for the woman to come home. The next-door neighbors, sensing something was amiss, intercepted her before she could fall victim and called the police.

The idiot boyfriend fled police in a dim-witted escape attempt that culminated with him jumping off the Ambassador Bridge when he saw that his escape to Canada was thwarted. The Coast Guard fished him out, he was tried and is now, as far as I know, rotting in prison serving a life sentence. Here again, this person could have just as easily attacked her in the workplace, but luck and convenience seems to be the only reason he did not,

There is a bias in our criminal justice system AGAINST pursuing domestic violence cases because too often the victim drops the charges, we need to work to change that and perhaps this book will inspire someone to take up the cause, but until then I hope this book protects people in the workplace.

intended to aid you in screening applicants who might be at risk of perpetrating a single shooter event in the workplace, and secondly, this book will help you to spot individuals who are likely to be targeted for this type of attack and by association put your workplace at risk.

This book is important because employers have a moral, ethical, and legal responsibility for keeping their workers safe, and homicide is the leading cause of workplace death for women. At no point should this book or the information therein be used to illegally discriminate against women who might be targeted but forewarned is forearmed and if you do knowingly hire a woman or man who is at high risk of being targeted you must take all necessary precautions to protect the individual and the company. Throughout this book I refer to the perpetrator as male, again, this is deliberate because women are at far greater risk of being murdered at work by a relative or a domestic partner and it is exponentially more likely that a man will be the killer.

The psychology behind this gender inequality is important, but frankly not as important as knowing that it is far more likely for female employees to be targeted than men. This statistic is somewhat misleading, as men tend to die in the workplace in greater numbers than women and men are disproportionately more likely to be employed doing high-risk work. But the statistic that cannot be ignored is that across all industries, in the US at very least, the incidence of death at the hands of a relative of domestic partner is a scant 2% for men, and a staggering 42% (the single largest category) for a woman. This is an issue that has been ignored for too long, and I intend to address it with all the snarkiness and rancor that it deserves. For statistics to be this far out of whack it means that companies aren't doing enough to protect women either out of ignorance or incompetence. After completing reading this book you can no longer plead ignorance, but I can't do anything to make you more competent. You will either use this book as a wakeup call or remain living in a bubble and put people at risk.

Percentage of Women Killed by Type of Assailant [4]

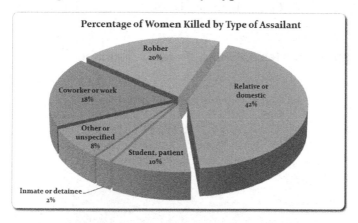

Nearly half of all women murdered in the workplace will be killed by a relative or a domestic partner, while only 2% of men will be killed in this way! Men fare far worse in robberies with 33% of the homicides resulting from this source as compared to women, but there little statistical difference between the gender of the victims and percentage of the homicides.

If this statistic alarms you, and it should, but remember that it is somewhat misleading. A single shooter event in the workplace motivated by a domestic dispute is likely to result in more than one victim. Often, a man coming to the aid of the intended target, or a man who is romantically involved with the victim is also a target but, does not fall into the same category. Unless the assailant is a coworker the man's death is likely to be categorized as "other or unspecified".

Additionally, nearly 18% of women are murdered by coworkers versus 15% for men. These attacks are most often motivated by a disgruntled worker who has been dismissed or about to be fired. Effectively this means that statistically it is

---

[4] *Source: https://www.bls.gov/iif/oshwc/cfoi/homicides2015-chart2data.htm*

about equal for a woman supervisor to be murdered by a unstable subordinate than it is for a man in a similar circumstances.

Percentage of Men Killed by Type of Assailant [5]

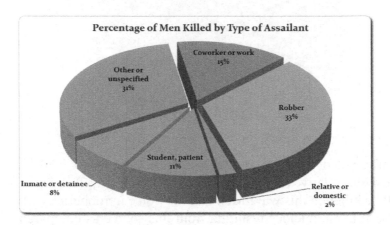

While women tend to be killed by family members or domestic partners, men on the other hand tend to be killed either by attempting to defend a woman or killed by an employee. In the chart above you see the marked increase in the category "as other or unspecified" (almost three times as likely as women) which COULD be attributed to attempts at defending a target or simply and innocent bystander

If we can rule out killings by inmates and other or unspecified (typically this refers to assailants who are not captured and their gender is unknown) we find that not only is the most common cause of workplace deaths for women homicides but for working outside of institutions these women are going to die at the hands of a relative or domestic partner.

What makes the single shooter event most shocking and terrifying is the ease with which it is carried out and the

---

[5] *Source: https://www.bls.gov/iif/oshwc/cfoi/homicides2015-chart2data.htm*

absolute ability for organizations to—with little effort—spot the warning signs and prevent workplace violence with minimal effort.

I should be clear here: while this is predominately a woman's issue it is far from exclusively women who are affected. Years ago, I went through a particularly ugly divorce. My wife left and moved in with her father (as close a facsimile to RP McMurphy as I think anyone is likely to find) between lines of coke my ex would come to my house while I was at work and treat it like her own personal Bed Bath and Beyond. (One trip she took all the spoons and bath towels). I got sick of it and changed the locks. She left me an incoherent message that I listened to in disgust until I heard her clearly say "I'm coming over there with my dad with his pistol and we're going to kill you and take what we want". Before I could get out of the door they were in the driveway. I called the police. She tried kicking the door in but when neighbors started watching they got spooked and fled the scene. The police arrived a short time later and told me to go somewhere they couldn't find me for a while and let things cool off. This was before domestic violence and stalking laws were updated to reflect the true threat level. I left with the clothes on my back, not wishing to endanger my family or friends I went on the lam and stayed at a filthy but cheap motel (the mold in the shower was so thick I swear it snarled at me and called me a punk). I won't disclose who took my daughter, but she was safe. So anytime anyone bad mouths a battered woman for staying I just tell them to live that life and you'll have all the answers. I had just the smallest of tastes of that nightmare and I didn't care for it even a little.

My ex and her father are both gone now victims, of, if not pioneers of, the opioid epidemic. I claimed her body bringing everything full circle.

Now when people ask me why I never remarried I just tell them that I did my time in hell. So, while I was never battered, she did her best to emotionally abuse me. Emotional abuse is real, it's not just an insult here and there, it chips away at your psyche until there very little fight left in you. You resign yourself that you are going to be miserable.

Unfortunately, it too often becomes physical, a push, a slap, until one day the abused person ends up on a gurney with a sheet over her head. Yes, this can happen to men, and in many ways it's far more difficult for men to deal with---society is far less sympathetic of the man who gets beat up by a girl.

But in many cases, a woman will enlist a new lover or family member to inflict the abuse. The wife of a man I know was cheating on him. He found out when he returned home to be ambushed by her new lover and his buddy who beat him unconscious with baseball bats. It seemed to me that moving out of the apartment and leaving a note would have sufficed, but then again, he was never very nice to me and I always thought he would benefit from a good and frothy ass beating. Even here my societal bias rears its ugly head, but I do have some sympathy for him; it's one thing to get punched in the nose and quite another to be set upon by bat wielding thugs in your own home.

In another case, my neighbor was ambushed on his way to work by two men (one of them his wife's lover) with shotguns. They blasted away and yet he survived with only minor injuries, and his wife and erstwhile hitmen all went to jail.

There. I shared stories of men being victims of domestic violence. So those of you reading this can shut your pie holes about me ignoring violence against men. These are a) actual true stories from my own experience or from experience of

people I know, and b) the common thread in these stories is that men played a key role in the violence.

Of course, there are men who are beaten by women because they refuse to fight back, but all of these cases are statistical outliers. The majority of men do not beat the women in their lives, and even fewer women abuse their domestic partners, so let's focus on the real issues and forget the political correctness.

It's worth considering a point made by many (mostly men) who point to the "fact" that men disproportionately perform more dangerous jobs than women and therefore are most certainly will be killed on the job by causes other than murder and therefore that skews the data. This isn't supported by any statistics that I could find. But it doesn't really matter. If I were writing a book about confined space deaths or some other cause of workplace deaths I wouldn't be talking about gender because no other cause of workplace deaths deliberately target a specific gender.

I also find it interesting that nobody brushes away the fact that men are disproportionately murdered during robberies. If we can be so quick to dismiss the gender disparity in workplace murders why don't we also dismiss the gender disparity in robberies? My guess is that many people believe that the victims of domestic abuse somehow deserve their fates; but that's just a guess.

I'm a bit jaded from spending nearly two decades in worker safety where in many situations blaming the victims is the name of the game.

Chapter 3: Preventing Workplace Violence

People are primates and primates are violent creatures. Any of you who have dated a chimp with a drinking problem knows how dangerous they can be. They also don't take criticism well, but that's for another book. Some of the men aren't that much different from chimps; push the wrong buttons and you end up with a broken jaw.

It is impossible to completely prevent workplace violence—the terrifying reality is if a madman wants to kill people in the workplace he will likely succeed and there is little you can do to stop a carefully planned and executed attack, but you can greatly reduce the risk of an incidence of workplace violence through some simple changes to your company policies.

Prevention begins with recruiting

Throughout this book I will use the pronoun "you". "You" could be a Human Resources Vice President, or 'you" could be a supervisor, or "you" could be a coworker, or "you" could be a potential victim. If YOU are too stupid to figure out whether or not I am talking to YOU then stop reading this book and pick up a copy of Curious George a book I have always enjoyed.

For those of you still reading, a good way to avoid a workplace shooting is to avoid hiring people who are unstable and/or who demonstrate a pattern of violent behavior. This is sometimes a lot more difficult than it seems. When I think back to the rogue's gallery of socially maladroit misfits with whom I have worked, I am shock that I haven't been gunned down, or at very least shot at while ran cravenly to hide under a desk or behind a file cabinet.

In this day where people blithely post on social media sometimes outrageous and ominously threatening statements that provide a hidden glimpse into their personalities, it's now easier than ever to legally gain information on an individual's mental state and volatility.

Even as individuals try to conceal embarrassing posts it is still possible to gain important insights. Here are some potential red flags that are worth considering, as you read through them remember there are two conditions for which you are screening 1) someone who is at high risk of committing workplace violence and 2) someone who is a likely victim of workplace violence: (**Note**: a company shouldn't dismiss a good candidate simply because of the presence of a single red flag—then again these red flags should be strongly considered before hiring (or even interviewing) a candidate:

- **Hate Speech.** This should be fairly obvious, but it can be surprisingly common for an individual to post an overt, or thinly veiled, racial slur, ethnic insults, or negative comments indicating bigotry toward one or more subpopulations. This isn't a call for people to be politically correct to a nauseating extent, but if a candidate is comfortable enough to attack a protected class in public posts, he or she probably lacks the

38

judgment that God gave geese, and ultimately these bigotries will likely manifest in the workplace.

- A person who posts or who allows his or her contacts to post hate speech comments unchallenged on his or her posts is also a red flag, as the adage goes, birds of a feather flock together. Seriously though is this really something a recruiter or hiring managers need to be told? With the amount of hate speech being posted and the number of the people who are posting it I have to conclude that yeah, they do.

Nothing I like more than when some mouth-breather works himself into a froth and starts spewing treats and insults at me. I simply respond with how much I admire their courage; to so openly and freely use pejorative language ,with complete confidence that their bosses, customers, potential employers, prospective customers, and romantic interests all share the feelings, and secretly applaud their open use of language typically reserved for a Klan rally. That generally gives them pause.

- **Belligerence.** Some people enjoy provoking others; I do, for example, but that is a major part of my job. I have to use provocation to move people out of their comfort zones (the irony of this particular bullet point is not lost on me) so that they can change. But the accounting clerk that you are considering probably isn't being belligerent to make the math work, so a belligerent tone or a pattern of belligerent posts should be weighed against the job and its requirements.

- **Volatility.** Even a saint can be pushed to the breaking point and post or say something that he or she wished he hadn't, but what can be really telling is when a shifts from mildly argumentative to the post a screaming frothy rage. This "flick a switch" going from zero to raging gaping maniac (not my first choice of word) is a strong red flag.

Even though we know that people often act in a way online that they would never act in person, they still secretly or silently harbor these feeling strongly enough to post them in a public forum and the right stimuli could set them off.

- **Obsession with guns.** This might seem obvious to some and unfair to others. I have a social contact who almost exclusively posts photos of automatic weapons. Another is a self-described gun nut. In and of themselves these two would seem to be people you don't want to hire. In fact, one of them is in ROTC and the other is an artist that draws weapons for a popular single-shooter video game and requires the guns for research for his job. Neither of them is belligerent or exhibit any violent tendencies; again these are indicators and have to be considered in a larger context with the other red flags and when taken with other red flags should be used in making an informed decision as to how to handle the individual.

- **Obsession with Violent Events.** Whenever there is a high-profile single shooter event the social networks are littered with posts relative to the event. But there are also individuals who post memes, articles, or statements that form a pattern that suggests if not an obsession with violence a keen interest in it. This behavior goes far beyond keeping up with current events and is clearly indicative of at very least a morbid curiosity with violence and at worst a propensity for violence.

- **Hostility toward an ex.** Personally, I don't trust anyone who has an amicable relationship with their ex-lover or ex-spouse. When people used to ask me if I was still friends with my ex-wife (she is since deceased, and no, I didn't have anything to do with it) I would say that if we were friends we would probably still be married, but that I bore her no ill feelings (which was true).

I've also have had ex-romantic entanglements who, when she broke it off, expressed an interest in remaining friends. I always say "no, I have enough friends and I would have to have a friend quit or die before I can make any additional friends; I can put you on a waitlist if you like." Inexplicably there have been no takers thus far. Even so I don't bear them any ill will, and when someone posts virulent, angry posts about how horrible a person his or her ex is, at very least you can glean a bit about their temperament, and/or the temperament of his or her ex.

- **It's Complicated Relationship Status.** Tread lightly here. In many countries, it is illegal to ask or to use as a criterion for hiring, a candidate's marital status, and that is not what I am suggesting. But the response, "it's complicated" could indicate marital strife, difficulties with an on-again-off-again partner, marriage to a semiaquatic mammal, or variety of things that should raise a red flag, but then again it could indicate a relationship that is completely innocuous and in no way predictive of workplace violence.

The point being is that any vagueness that could indicate a propensity for future workplace violence needs to be considered, but merely considered for the purposes of future heightened awareness should you hire the person, not as a criterion for such a hire.

- **Excessive alcohol use.** Is there a preponderance of posts of alcohol use? Does the candidate proudly post the details (at least what they can remember) or the previous weekend bender? Are the pictures disproportionately of alcoholic drinks or of social events where alcohol is served? Does the candidate often check in at bars or parties?

In most of the workplace violence episodes, alcohol is usually involved. The perfect formula for a workplace single shooter event is unhappy relationship + quick access to a firearm + mental illness with violent tendency + alcohol.

- **An overall negative outlook.** Everybody gets negative once in a while, but as you read through a candidate's posts do they seem overly angry, depressed, or just see the world as filled with personal injustices and unpleasantness? If so, how qualified does Eeyore have to be for you to say, "gosh darn it, this candidate's post makes ME depressed, but I still want 'em on my team?"

Negativity can be contagious and it can spread with alarming speed, also, a person with a negative outlook is also less resilient which correlates to more absenteeism, and difficulty rebounding from personal or professional setbacks. Even if the person isn't a potential killer, who wants to have this person at the company picnic?

- **No social media presence.** In an age when grandparents have Facebook pages and Twitter accounts it is practically unheard of for someone under the age of 70" to not have a social media presence. If someone doesn't have a social media account, it may indicate that they have deleted the account or are using a pseudonym. This is hardly damning; the person may merely want to get rid of the public displays of youthful indiscretions.

Personally, I don't see why my Facebook page is festooned with posts of me drinking, spewing obscenities (some of which I made up (patent pending...fingers crossed)) and dubious check-ins. But I like people to have a good idea who they're dealing with, plus as an author who is known for his poison-pen and tongue dripping venom, I get away with a lot more than most.

As for your average candidate, again, it shouldn't be a deal breaker but should be considered another possible indicator. If you were considering bringing me aboard when you started reading you probably have since changed your mind.

Again, none of these things in itself identifies a dangerous individual but it provides an important piece of the puzzle that you really need when you hire a person, and you need that information BEFORE you bring the person in for an interview.

All this sounds like a lot of work, and it can be, but it is far less time consuming and gut wrenching as telling the loved ones of someone murdered in your workplace that you could have prevented the death but it was just too darned much work.

I've heard arguments that social media is protected speech and a person has every right to post whatever he or she pleases. It's a fair point, but people too often believe that freedom of speech includes protection from the consequences of spewing malodorous dreck from your mouth.

You do have the right to say (within limits) what you want. Most people don't read the social networks' terms of services and these terms of service often severely curtail what you can and can't say. Even if social networks didn't have this in place there is nothing protecting you from people thinking you're an asshat.

Of all the rights that people choose to exercise sadly, too few exercise the right to remain silent.

Privacy versus Safety

I'm sure I am not alone in this when I say, "to hell with your privacy" when I am trying to protect the workplace from potentially unstable murderous maniacs, but I confess to being a bit more reluctant to pry into the personal lives. Looking at posts on social media once an individual has been hired should only be done if there is cause (and should follow all applicable laws). That having been said what constitutes "cause"?

- Worker or customer complaints. Certainly, a complaint from a coworker or a customer should prompt you to monitor the individual in question's social media posts.
- Bizarre behavior. If a worker engages in behavior that strikes you as unusually bizarre you might want to take a peek into their cyber stronghold.
- Signs of violence. People can be amazingly stupid in what they post. They may proudly post of bashing in the face of the ex's new boyfriend on social media.

Background Checks

44

Before we get into background checks we should review the U.S. Federal Equal Opportunity Commission has to say on the subject, because, let's face it, violating the law is wrong even when the intent is to protect your workers. The EOC says[6]: "Federal law does not prohibit employers from asking about your criminal history. But, federal EEO laws do prohibit employers from discriminating when they use criminal history information. Using criminal history information to make employment decisions may violate Title VII of the Civil Rights Act of 1964, as amended (Title VII).

- Title VII prohibits employers from treating people with similar criminal records differently because of their race, national origin, or another Title VII-protected characteristic (which includes color, sex, and religion).

- Title VII prohibits employers from using policies or practices that screen individuals based on criminal history information if:

  o They significantly disadvantage Title VII-protected individuals such as African Americans and Hispanics; AND
  o They do not help the employer accurately decide if the person is likely to be a responsible, reliable, or safe employee."

Okay, so another disclaimer, I am not a lawyer. But having said that, what this means is that you have every right to ask about criminal history, restraining orders, arrests, etc. as long as you don't ask one protected class more frequently than another. So IF you look into someone's criminal and arrest records you should be prepared that you are doing it for ALL candidates for that position and can defend against claims that you are singling out someone because of their race, religion, country of origin, or similar protected class, AND to do the investigation in a

---

[6] *Source: https://www.eeoc.gov/laws/practices/inquiries_arrest_conviction.cfm*

good faith effort to ensure the safety of your employees, which given the context of this investigation, i.e. to reduce the risk of hiring someone with a history of violent behavior that could spill over into the workplace should not be hard to do.

Let's face it, if you were to close your eyes and picture your average domestic abuser your picture would likely be wrong. The fact is, except for the fact that the population is overwhelmingly male, there it is nearly impossible to identify a domestic abuser by looks alone.

In the rush to fill a position some employers will skip background checks. A background check is an important step in the hiring process. Some companies, citing the expense of doing a background check, will only do background checks on candidates who are above a certain pay grade. Ironically, the incidences of disgruntled executives returning to a workplace to kill indiscriminately are all but unheard of. When considering the expense of a background check, consider the cost of having a sociopath on the payroll. Companies can never underestimate the dangers of skipping background checks. Background checks should include:

- **Court Records.** Does the candidate have a restraining order against him or her, or has the candidate filed for a restraining order against someone else? This is easy information to obtain and it is a big red flag that the candidate is either capable of violence or has a history with someone who is potentially dangerous. Incidents of domestic abuse should be given particular scrutiny as they are often a causative factor in workplace violence.

- **Arrest Record.** Has the candidate been arrested (but perhaps not charged) for violent crimes, particularly for domestic violence? Why domestic violence? Let's not forget that a leading cause of workplace fatalities is domestic disputes and more likely than not the woman associated with the case will be a victim.

46

There is a National Domestic Abuse registry available on-line   https://www.domesticviolencedatabase.net/ This is a good source of information as to whether a candidate has been involved in child abuse/spousal abuse/elder abuse etc. This research isn't about discriminating against women who have already been victimized, but it IS about understanding with whom you are dealing.

A target of violence outside of work is likely to be a victim of violence INSIDE of work. The victim will require extra protection and you need to take precautions. You need to be sensitive to the target's privacy, but you must balance that against the legitimate safety of her coworkers. It's a horrible position to turn someone down for a position that is ill advised and perhaps illegal, simply because she has been victimized, but you have to balance that against your obligation to the other member of your workforce and their right to be safe.

- **Criminal Record**. Just because a person has a criminal record doesn't mean that the person is prone to violence, however, if the person has lied about his or her criminal conviction it is an indicator of the person's character.

Note: the EOC has different rules governing arrest and conviction records:

"Difference Between Arrest Records and Conviction Records

The fact that an individual was arrested is not proof that he engaged in criminal conduct. Therefore, an individual's arrest record standing alone may not be used by an employer to take a negative employment action (e.g., not hiring, firing or suspending an applicant or employee). However, an arrest may trigger an inquiry into whether the conduct underlying the arrest justifies such action.

In contrast, a conviction record will usually be sufficient to demonstrate that a person engaged in particular criminal conduct. In certain circumstances, however, there may be reasons for an employer not to rely on the conviction record alone when making an employment decision.

Several states' laws limit employers' use of arrest and conviction records to make employment decisions. These laws may prohibit employers from asking about arrest records or require employers to wait until late in the hiring process to ask about conviction records. If you have questions about these kinds of laws, you should contact your state fair employment agency for more information. For more information on the laws governing criminal background checks go to: https://www.eeoc.gov/eeoc/newsroom/wysk/arrest_co nviction_records.cfm[7]

- **History of Incarceration.** Even individuals who have been incarcerated for non-violent offenses can often become indoctrinated into a culture of violence as a direct result of prolonged incarceration. This is not to say that you shouldn't hire an ex-convict, however, it is another indicator that the person may have violent tendencies, and you need to consider this in the context of all facets of the person's personality and background. I could go on and on about the many convicted felons who went on to become sterling citizens but then this book isn't intended to protect you from reformed convicts into Jean Valjean; if you are looking for that read *Les Miserables*.

---

[7] https://www.eeoc.gov/laws/practices/inquiries_arrest_conviction.cfmn

48

- **Employment History.** Are their significant gaps in the person's work history? These could indicate incarceration or commitment to a mental institution. Do the companies seem reticent about discussing the circumstances of the person's departure from the company? If possible talk to the candidate's manager; he or she will likely be candid regarding whether or not the candidate is capable of committing workplace violence. Be careful not to put too much stock in a single gap or even several short gaps. Some people leave toxic work environments or because they fear that a co-worker could be a target (or perpetrator) and decide to quit his or her job despite not having another job already secured, But at the risk of sounding repetitive (did I say that already?) this is an indicator in a long line of indicators.

- **Credit History.** Credit checks are an increasingly common part of the background check, and it can provide important clues to potential perpetrators or victims of a single shooter event. Money problems rank very high in the list of causes of marital or nontraditional spousal partnership problems and are quite often a trigger for domestic violence. But if you are going to use this information to ascertain criminal acts you should be aware of the EOC's Consumer Protections and Criminal Background Checks:

  "Employers that obtain an applicant's or employee's criminal history information from consumer reporting agencies (CRAs) also must follow the Fair Credit Reporting Act (FCRA). For example, FCRA requires employers to:

  - Get your permission before asking a CRA for a criminal history report;

- Give you a copy of the report and a summary of your rights under FCRA before taking a negative employment action based on information in the report.

- Send you certain notices if it decides not to hire or promote you based on the information in the CRA report.[8-9]

Don't take too much stock in credit scores as a single indicator. My credit score is so bad that it's actually good protection from identity thieves, in that nobody wants to be me; all that gets you is ass beatings and debt.

- **References.** Some people view asking for references as a waste of time, after all, what kind of social misfit would give the names of someone who will give them a bad reference? Precisely the kind who might shoot up your office and destroy that snow globe your boss brought you back from his trip to Des Moines (don't expect the cheap bastard to replace it). I have checked references for candidates only to find out that the person listed as a reference didn't know or gave an out-and-out bad reference for the person. Ask the reference about how the candidate handles stress or even if they believe that either the candidate is capable of violence or if there is anyone in the candidate's life that might be violent and wish to the harm the candidate. Anonymity breeds candor.

---

[8] *If you would like to know more about FCRA, visit the Federal Trade Commission's (FTC) website (the federal agency that enforces FCRA). Or contact the FTC at 1-877-FTC-HELP (1-877-832-4357); TTY: 1-866-653-4261.*

[9] *https://www.eeoc.gov/laws/practices/inquiries_arrest_conviction.cfm*

- **Google search.** It's always surprising how much information you can get from a simple search on the web. As a reporter and contributor to numerous magazines I have something of a reputation for being able to quickly and accurately get information; my prowess was the thing of myths. My secret? Google. I don't pay for information but it's not a bad idea to do so.

  Remember to dig deep in your google searches, professional reputational cleaners will simply add so much new information that a person's arrest for having carnal knowledge with a dead raccoon will be so deeply buried that unless you google "sex"+"dead raccoon" you're not likely to find it.

- **Drug screening.** It may surprise you, but fewer and fewer companies are requiring random drug testing. The reason given is that they so seldom catch offenders that it's difficult

I work for five different clients that require my firm to randomly test for drugs. I joke that I keep a mason jar of pee in my refrigerator because I get "randomly" selected (it just saves time).

Interviewing a candidate

Interviewing a candidate is the best way to get to know them in a short amount of time. The person's timeliness, dress, mannerisms, tone of voice, and just your gut feeling about a candidate may prove invaluable. In addition to the questions, you would normally ask, you should ask questions that provide you with insight into the person's personality. Ask open-ended questions like the following to gain information that you can use legally and ethically to avoid hiring someone who will likely engage in workplace violence or make your company a target for a single shooter event. I literally could write a book about the stupid things people say in job interviews.

I once had a candidate send me an email angergram that he tried unsuccessfully to pull back, it didn't change anything, he was a controlling, unpleasant, know-it-all puss bag who I wouldn't hire on a dare knowing that I was quitting the next day. He was angry because we administered a common and valid personality inventory as part of the screening process. There were no right or wrong answers, but I was looking for someone whose personality would be different enough from my own to offer the learners different styles of instruction. I don't remember the details, but the tone was angry, and he called me everything but a child of God. It appears he was less than a fan of said personality inventory. Seriously, I wonder to this day, what this dim bulb expected to accomplish through this email that he sent but tried to unsend. In the long run I guess it doesn't matter, but if I WAS going to hire him, that would have certainly changed my mind.

Keep in mind that one of the most difficult things in a job interview is determining whether or not the person is a duplicitous, pathological liar. In his June 2016 article for *Psychology Today*, *6 Ways to Detect a Liar*, Dr. Gregory L. Jantz offers some insightful ways to tell if someone is being completely truthful.

According to Jantz, 80% of lies go undetected" but if that is true can we really believe him? Jantz asserts that the all too common practice of a child lying about eating candy before dinner (and presumably other inconsequential untruths) set the pattern for lying in later life. "This opportunity-cost process that children go through to avoid getting in trouble sets the foundation for a pattern of lying in the future" notes Jantz, and while Jantz claims that "people will always get away with lying, most lies are pretty easy to spot if you know how to read the signs."

Jantz suggests that we start by asking some neutral questions, by this he means questions that all, but the most sociopathic creeps would answer truthfully. "By asking someone basic, non-threatening questions, you are able to observe a response baseline. Ask them about the weather, their plans for the weekend, or anything that would elicit a normal, comfortable response. When they respond, observe their body language and eye movement—you want to know how they act when they are telling the truth. Do they shift stance? Glance in one direction or the other? Or look you dead in the eye? Make sure you ask enough questions to observe a pattern" says Jantz. A baseline reading on the person is important for you to be able to distinguish their nervous tics and natural body language and tone of voice from changes that may indicate deceit.

Next, Jantz recommends you "find the hot spot". The hot spot is where people become uncomfortable telling the absolute truth and while different people may have different "tells" (things they do unconsciously or even physiological changes in the body) that indicates that their stress is increased, which often accompanies a lie. "Once you move from neutral territory to the "lie zone," you should be able to observe a change in body language, facial expressions, eye movement, and sentence structure. Everyone will give different subconscious clues when telling a lie, which is why it's important to observe a normal baseline prior to entering the lie zone," according to Jantz.

Jantz's third tip is one I often share and in which I strongly believe: "Watch body language." This is easy to do, but what exactly does a liar's body language look like? Jantz believes " Liars often pull their body inward when lying to make themselves feel smaller and less noticeable. Many people will become squirmy and sometimes conceal their hands to subconsciously hide fidgety fingers. You might also observe shoulder shrugging." It's important to remember that body language can mean different things in different contexts and it needs to be viewed holistically. As noted clinical psychologist and study of the psychology of nonverbal communication often said, "sometimes arms folded tightly across a person's chest can indicate defensiveness, in other cases it could mean the person is cold, and in still other cases it could just be a comfortable way to sit or stand."

It takes more concentration to lie, and this effort is hard to mask. Jantz advises us to "Observe micro-facial expressions. People will often give away a lie in their facial expression, but

54

some of these facial expressions are subtle and difficult to spot. Some people will change the facial coloration to a slighter (sic) shade of pink, others will flare their nostrils slightly, bite their lip (sic) perspire slightly, or blink rapidly. Each of these changes signifies an increase in brain" activity as lying begins."

Another tip that Jantz offers is to: "Listen to tone, cadence, and sentence structures." This is again why having a baseline reading of the person is so important. Jantz reminds us that, "Often when a person is lying, they will slightly change the tone and cadence of their speech. They might start speaking more quickly or slowly, and with either a higher or lower tone. Often, the sentences they use become more complex as their brain works on overdrive to keep up with their tale."

And finally, Jantz offers this tip on the subject of lying, "Watch for when they stop talking about themselves.

People who are lying will also sometimes start removing themselves from their story, and start directing the focus on other people. You will hear fewer Me's and I's as liars try to psychologically distance themselves from the lie that they're weaving."

Perhaps most important in Jantz advice is his one caveat: Remember: Everyone has different 'lying behavior' so there is no one guaranteed lie-detection method. It's most important to be able to compare a liar's baseline behavior to the body movement, facial expressions, eye movement, and verbal cues that they use when they are telling a lie.[10]

Even if you aren't a big fan of psychology, the physiological responses one unconsciously exhibits while lying. In her March 2009, WebMD Article, *10 Ways to Catch a Liar*, Heather Hatfield cites top experts in lie detection that largely echo Jantz's observations. Hatfield starts with a tip from J.J. Newberry, a federal agent "skilled in the art of deception de-

---

[10] Source: *https://www.psychologytoday.com/us/blog/hope-relationships/201507/6-ways-detect-liar-in-just-seconds*

tection." Hatfield tells the story of Newberry unraveling a witness's attempt at deception by his recognition of "tell tales signs that a person isn't being honest like inconsistencies in a story, behavior that's different from a person's norm, or too much detail in an explanation" (by the way if you go by that last one everything I say is a lie. I am a compulsive explainer.)

Hatfield takes pains to remind us that it takes years of training to reach the expertise of J.J. Newberry, however, she does offer useful tips for detecting deceptions. "Look for inconsistencies" I didn't need this article to tell me that. I watch Judge Judy daily and pray that you don't come knocking on my door when I'm watching my stories; seriously I will mess you up.

Judge Judy (for those of you who have been living under a rock for the last ten years or so) is a show where retired Judge Judith Sheindlin metes out justice to dimwits seriously too stupid to watch her show before appearing on it. She yells at people, she calls them stupid, and even offered to explain to one unfortunate, "why he is an idiot." Judge Judy is a human lie detector and one of her favorite tactics is to find inconsistencies in people's testimony. She'll say things like, "that's not what you told me a moment ago" or "that's not what you said in your answer". Being called on their inconsistencies seems to trigger other tells so obvious that even I can spot them as lying pieces of excrement. Judge Judy also is fond of saying that if something doesn't make sense then it isn't true".

Another thing that Judge Judy does to expose a liar is to ask seemingly unrelated questions, in a job interview the questions are usually arranged in a logical hierarchy, basic small talk, followed by questions organized around the resume, questions about work history, etc. but if you want to find out if the person is a liar, mix up that order and ask something seemingly out of the blue to trip up the person; that may seem ridiculous, but remember we want to sort the liars and violent potential attackers from good candidates who will generally do their best to stay on track and be honest; it may feel like dirty pool, but then doesn't the liar deserve it?

Judge Judy also uses another technique to expose a liar, which is to ask seemingly unrelated questions, again in a job interview the questions are usually arranged in a logical hierarchy, basic small talk, followed by questions organized around the resume, questions about work history, etc. but if you want to find out if the person is a liar, mix up that order and ask something seemingly out of the blue to trip up the person; that may ridiculous, but remember we want to sort the liars and violent potential attackers from good candidates who will generally do their best to stay on track and be honest.

Another thing you can do to both throw the liar off his or her game is to paraphrase what they have told you and point out where it is inconsistent with other things he or she has said. I once had a woman show up 55 minutes late for a job interview. She came in and promptly plopped a 64-ounce sweating plastic cup of soda on my desk. I asked her why she was late to which she promptly and adeptly concocted a fable that would make Aesop himself weep with envy. She told an elaborate tale of a horrific highway crash that closed all lanes giving minute details and finally finished with a melodramatic, "I got here as soon as I could...I couldn't even get off the freeway to call.

I paraphrased her story back to her and ended with, "what I am a bit unclear about is how you managed to stop at a convenience store and buy that soda but couldn't stop to call me." Her story fell apart and as much as I tried to get past it I just could shake the feeling that she was a compulsive liar.

Speaking of compulsive liars, my daughter once told me that I wouldn't have to preface my conversations with "this is a true story if I didn't lie so much", but then again, if I DID lie less think of how much less you could learn about lying from me.

Have you ever lied to someone that was interviewing you for a position? If you are like most people you have, and if you are telling yourself you never have you are probably lying right now. According to a study, UK job seekers found that over half the applicants admitted lying on their CV and a staggering 75% felt that it was their bosses' responsibility to uncover the lie, and an astonishing 91% said their bosses never found out.[11]

I get this, I routinely tell people interviewing me that I used to be the U.S Ambassador of Grease (that's not a typo, I claimed that I was the ambassador to an off-Broadway production and not the country. It was impossible to disprove and may have been the perfect lie).

The fact of the matter is that people will say most anything to get that coveted job offer, and what's more, many more will lie on their resume, and even more will lie on Social Media---Hell my Facebook page says I graduated from Harvard (I graduated from the University of Michigan Dearborn, considered the Harvard of Dearborn) and that I work as an Evangelist at the digital Bible. If you can't lie to your friends that you don't care enough about to call on the phone, then seriously who CAN you lie to?

As I researched this book, I got interested in what the most common lies told during job interviews (not counting the filthy, filthy, lies told by recruiters and hiring managers.) I came across this gem "The 10 Most Common Lies That Job Candidates Will Tell You" by Mark Wilkenson https://www.coburgbanks.co.uk/blog/assessing-applicants/10-common-lies-job-candidates-tell/ This article is an invaluable resource for constructing questions that you know people are likely to lie about and therefore are useful for identifying how people react when they are lying. Remember, by asking baseline questions followed by questions that almost all applicants lie about you will get a feeling for those micro

---

[11] *https://www.recruiter.co.uk/news/2015/06/half-jobseekers-admit-lying-their-cv-beat-their-competition-job*

expressions that last but a fraction of a moment but are incredibly strong predictors of deception. So, what does Mark Wilkinson assert as the most common lies?

1) Employment dates. I can understand why people want to cover up gaps in employment, while many people are laid off for short periods of time, quit before finding another job, or just plain leave a toxic work environment, but to the intern sorting the resumes it looks like they spent a month at burning man smoking hash with Gary Busey. This is completely unfair, because even Gary Busey couldn't smoke THAT much hash and even if he could where would he get enough time to party with all those people? The truth is many, perhaps most people have employment gaps that are easily explained, but candidates often worry that any gaps in employment will disqualify them before they have an opportunity to explain.

"So" according to Wilkinson, "those who have gaps that aren't easy to explain are left with two choices: trying to tell the truth in a more appealing way on their CV and possibly not even getting a call back for jobs or risk it, lie, and hope for the best."

According to Wilkinson, the second most common lie is, their educations. This is a lie that I know firsthand is shockingly common. Years ago when I had just transitioned from working the assembly line to a white color position, after being encouraged to explore other career opportunities.

I was (after a substantial gap in employment---or not---I was laid off from my employer, but still collecting unemployment, still collecting supplemental pay, and still on the company roll, all that I was no longer doing was working, which truth be told I didn't do much anyway, so I honestly don't know if I was employed or unemployed, plus I was doing side work (and declaring it and paying my taxes) so I honestly don't know if there was a gap or not.)

I was employed at a construction management company as head of Training. (Not all that big a deal considering I was a department of one) there wasn't much training to be done since it was a startup department, so I was asked to help out doing background checks. In my unscientific, statistically invalid research, I found about 30% of the people lied about their education. Of that about 10% claimed to have earned Master's Degrees when they did not, another 70% attended the school in question but never finished their degrees and 10% who never attended at all.

I know a very successful business woman who reached the level of Vice President by (in part) claiming to have graduated a University she never attended. And true to form, nobody at the several businesses at which she worked ever found out the truth.

Wilkinson cites lying about one's skills as the third most common lie, in fact, he states "57% of job candidates embellish their skill set, to help them get a job.

That's pretty outrageous, isn't it?[12]

---

[12] *His words not mine. For all I know he's lying, after all, 63% of all statistics are made up.*

I don't know if I would call that outrageous. I speak four languages: English, Spanish, French, and Hungarian. I always thought that I spoke the languages fairly well until I went to a job interview where the person interviewing me was fluent in Hungarian, having spent several years as head of the firm's Hungarian office.

He greeted me in Hungarian and asked me how my flight was. I recognized the language AS Hungarian but had long since lost a sufficient lexicon to respond appropriately. I simply apologized and told him truthfully that my flight was fine, but unfortunately my Hungarian was a bit south of rusty.

Was I lying? I don't think so, in fact, I don't think I was exaggerating, but clearly my claim that I spoke "conversational Hungarian" was no longer true. I would say that the more technical the skill the less likely the candidate is to lie about proficiency in the skill, but I can't because, "I know some dolts who have lied about being proficient in complex and dangerous equipment that they never even heard of before applying for a position."

I once interviewed a candidate for a position of an instructional development. He had claimed on his resume experience in developing technology-based courses, an area that, while not a job requirement, was a skill set I was very interested in developing. I asked him to tell me about it. He went on describe a "training course" that he had developed for Lotus. I was suitably impressed---after all this is a subject matter that had a substantial skill set that needed to be mastered.

I asked him what language he programmed it in and he told me English. So, I clarified my question by asking what programming language. I asked a couple of questions and finally asked if he had written a computer-based program or a job aid (a simple reminder for basic tasks) he stared at me blankly and said, "I guess I don't know the difference". He wasn't malicious, he was (and probably remains) a dope. (When I asked him if he had any questions for me, he asked, "what happens if I just don't show up?" I was confused and seriously wondering if I was the victim of a practical joke, but I had to answer in good faith.

I sought clarification, "do you mean what would happen if you had an emergency and were unable to call in?" He in all earnestness said, "no, I mean like what if I just don't feel like coming to work one day and I just don't show up?" I explained our no-call/no show policy and hastily did my best to usher him out the door.

This guy was and is an imbecile. Whoever helped him falsify his resume did him no favors. So, lying about skills may not be true dishonesty it could be overconfidence, a misunderstanding of the nomenclature used to describe the skill, or just out-and-out stupidity.

Wilkinson asserts that the next most common lie is salary, and while it's true that people feel pressured into inflating their salary, I have to ask is it really a lie? Consider this: salary could mean my base pay, that is my yearly or hourly pay. Or my salary could be interpreted as my base wage plus the value of the benefits provided. In short there is so much gray area here that I would have a rough time calling someone a liar for calculating their compensation differently than I do.

Wilkinson's next category of lies, Weaknesses is probably the best way to get an accurate read on the micro-expressions, or as I like to call them "tells". When I read this, I thought of the episode of The Simpsons where Homer having gotten Marge pregnant with Bart had to get a grown-up job. The Nuclear

Plant was hiring so he applied. Smithers, the assistant to the plant owner, is conducting the interviews and since there are three candidates for two jobs, he decides to interview them all simultaneously. Smithers asks the question, "what is your greatest weakness:" The first candidate quickly and confidently says that he drives himself too hard, the second candidate with equal vigor says that he's a bit of a perfectionist, and then Homer slowly says (and I'm paraphrasing) "well...I'm not too bright, and I'm kind of a goofball, and after a while little things start "disappearing from the office" To which an incredulous Smithers says, "I only asked for one!"

The scene is comic because if you ask someone to describe a weakness as like as not you will get one of the first two answers. The intended audience for Wilkinson's article is made up of recruiters, and while Wilkinson weakly suggests that the recruiter could ask the question tougher, like, "yes, but that's not really a weakness is it? Could you give us another answer?" Wilkinson doesn't see much value in the question and outside the context of determining the liar's tells on the face of it he might be right. But what if confronting obvious lie could be used to provoke the candidate into a snotty or aggressive response?

Who would you hire? the person who responds in a sarcastic, "well I'm beginning to think answering stupid questions is one of my weaknesses" or "I'm sorry I really can't think of any" or "I know this is a standard answer, but wouldn't it be a better use of our time for me to tell you where I have the greatest opportunity to learn, or frame the question in some other, less negative way?" The first response may denote an ill-tempered jerk who can't even manage to hold it together long enough to get through an interview. The second response belies someone who is either too non-assertive to speak up (and therefore a potential target) OR so obliviously non-self-aware that he or she doesn't know his or her limitations, while the third answer, which I have actually successfully used, turns the question on its ear, demonstrates an awareness of the question's intent, but also makes no attempt to deceive the asker. (I didn't get the job because the recruiter didn't know his rectum from a jelly donut, but I AM NOT BITTER).

I'm not going to go through all of Wilkinson's lies because I frankly think he should have selected the top five and stuck with them, but there is one more I think is worth addressing: References. Whether or not someone is lying about a reference.

One might ask how valuable the answer is to an employer and decide that only a syphilitic baboon would provide anything less than sterling references, but here the lie is the big lie.

Many people fudge the relationship and instead of providing business contacts they provide family, friends, or neighbors. LinkedIn has added a new element to this. I now receive about three requests a month for referrals from people I have never met, and apart from being connected (if someone is a fan of my work my ego will not turn them away) on the site I don't know a single thing about them. For all I know they could live with a blow-up doll that they have so badly abused that it can only talk about it in a therapist office using, I assume, smaller blow up dolls. And people, myself included, will ask people to be their references without really knowing what questions will be asked or how the reference will be answered.

 One of my references, when asked my weakness, said, "Sometimes Phil gets impatient with people who don't see his genius soon enough." Of all the weaknesses he could have chosen, and they are legion and the things of prurient legends, he chose this. After it worked it got me the job, but then the dullards who hired me were surprised that I am INDEED impatient with the mouth-breathing dolt's indifference to my genius. Why ask a question if you aren't going to do anything with the information?

My favorite story about lying about references on a job application was from the *Mary Tyler Moore Show* when perpetual clueless boob anchorman, Ted Baxter, used Jacques Cousteau as a reference because he reasoned would be impossible to get a hold of. Makes sense to me.

Planning Your interviews

When you plan your interviews arrange the questions in four categories: Baseline questions, "hotspot questions", integrity questions, and job suitability questions.

Baseline Questions

Baseline questions are questions that are innocuous and only pathological liars would bother to lie about. When asking baseline questions, you should be carefully observing the subject's body language, mannerisms, and micro-expressions so that you will be able to detect changes in these things when they start lying like their pants are on fire.

Good baseline questions include:

Question: How do you like this weather?

Analysis: A neutral question like this puts the person at ease, or at least enough at ease so that you can get a sense of his or her default mannerisms and nonverbal messaging.

Question: Did you have any trouble finding us?

Analysis: Be careful when you ask people this question, they may be so much in "interview mode" that they may actually interpret this question as a test of their ability to follow directions and lie about the difficulty they had finding your location. Keep your tone of voice upbeat and non-accusatory.

67

Keep your questions neutral---no talk of politics, sports, or anything controversial; just keep it light and stick to topics of conversation you might have while waiting in line for a bus.

Hotspot Questions

Hotspot Questions are the questions that most people will lie about. By carefully observing their physical reactions and comparing them to the baseline questions you will have a good idea of their tells (the physiological changes that indicate that they are lying). Here are some good hotspot questions.

Question: I noticed that on your resume that you have never had a gap between positions, is that accurate? If so, how do you account for your success, and if not, why did you lie on your resume?

Analysis: In more cases than not, the individual a) has gaps where they were without work, often for good cause, but we are indoctrinated into thinking that gaps in employment are unforgivable. By forcing them into a position where they will either have to come clean (extremely unlikely) or bolster the lie with extraneous details, they will likely concoct an elaborate web of deceit all the while showing you their liar's tells

Question: Describe for me a situation when you were fired. How did that make you feel?

Analysis: Even if this person has never been fired, he or she will likely react. In this case the fewer the details the more honest the answer. For example, if the respondent says, "I've never been fired, but I was laid off. It made me feel unhappy" is likely a more truthful answer than "I wasn't actually fired, but there was an instance where my coworker was stealing, and the boss accused the entire night shift of stealing $34 out of the till. I told him that I didn't like being accused because I'm not a thief and besides I didn't even have access to the register. Things got a little heated, and I admit that I may have raised my voice to him. He accused me of being disrespectful and I told him that I thought HE was the one being disrespectful, and I quit." The former is to the point and not overly emotional, while the latter provides a tapestry of details that are neither necessary nor all that interesting. What this person carefully as he or she will likely be giving away all their non-verbal cues and liar's tells.

Question: Do you have any reason to believe that you could be targeted for violence?

Analysis: There is nothing quite like cutting to the quick (no pun intended) when asking about the possibility of workplace violence. If the person seems uncomfortable or takes a long time carefully choosing his or her words, it could indicate that he or she believes that he or she might well be targeted for violence and is uncomfortable answering truthfully.

Integrity Questions

Integrity questions are designed to provide insights into the character of the candidate. Obviously, you will want to have a good idea of the liar's tells when asking these questions. In this case the WAY in which the person answers the question is far more important than the answer itself (with some obvious exceptions). Integrity questions sound like this:

Some good questions to ask include:

Question: Tell me about a situation where you had a difficulty in a relationship (that could be a personal or professional relationship) where the other person was uncooperative. How did you handle that?

Analysis: A truly unstable individual will usually talk about problems with a coworker or a boss, but sometimes a candidate, particularly younger candidates without extensive work professional experience, will talk about conflict with a friendship or love interest. As the candidate answers the question, be alert to his or her body language. Does the question make the individual uncomfortable? Does the tone of the individual's voice change and become aggressive? Does the individual avoid the conflict or talk about a passive-aggressive response? A candidate's body language and tone of voice often can belie either a violent personality or a passive personality; the former is a red flag for obvious reasons and the latter is dangerous because a person who has passive, or passive-aggressive, personality is more likely to be a victim of domestic violence [12] and thus put your organization at a higher risk of becoming a target of a single shooter event.

---

[12] *Warning Signs by Matthew J. Geiger, The Washington Outsider*

Question: Do you have any reason to believe that you could be targeted for violence?

Analysis: There is nothing quite like cutting to the quick (no pun intended) when asking about the possibility of workplace violence. If the person seems uncomfortable or takes a long time carefully choosing his or her words it could indicate that he or she believes that he or she might well be targeted for violence and is uncomfortable answering truthfully.

Question: Tell me about the circumstances of the departure from your last employer?

Analysis: People tend to rehearse job interviews and are likely to have a pat answer for "why did you leave your last employer?", or "why are you looking to leave your current employer?" by asking the question in this way, the applicant is forced to tell you a story, and that story will likely provide you with far more information and far richer details than the pat answer. Don't be afraid to ask the applicant follow up questions like, "describe your relationship with your boss" or "was your boss supportive of your decision to leave?" or even questions like "what did you like most about your former employer?" or "what did you dislike most about your former employer?" These kinds of probing questions will give you greater insight into the applicant's interpersonal skills. Don't settle for pat answers like "it was a bad fit". Instead, follow up with the question, "why was it a bad fit?" or "what makes you think it was a bad fit?

Question: Tell me about a time when you were involved in an instance of bullying. How did you handle that?

Analysis: A candidate may honestly never have encountered a bully in a professional setting but most of us have been bullied or have bullied someone at some point in our lives. If the candidate avoids the question, for example, they might say, "I don't think I have encountered any bullying" then broaden the question, by saying "certainly you must have some experience, perhaps as a child, or where you witnessed a bullying situation; talk to me about that." If the person still claims that they have no experience with bullying, you will have to judge whether or not the person is being truthful or is trying to avoid an uncomfortable answer. Again, here is a situation where the candidate's body language will likely provide key cues as to whether or not they are being truthful.

Question: If a stranger was able to view your social media pages, what conclusions would they likely draw about you?

Analysis: Recently, a friend told me that a potential employer asked her to provide her Facebook page. I am not crazy about this because asking for it outright seems rude and overly intrusive, and employers need to remember that the recruiting and screening process is as much about the prospect deciding whether or not your organization is a place by which they wish to be employed as it is about whether or not you wish to employ a candidate. By asking the candidate what conclusions a stranger might make based on his or her social media presence you are able to see the person through their own lens, albeit a likely filtered lens. This not only tells you how the individual sees his or herself but also forces the individual to reflect on how the world sees him or her; this can often suss out feelings of persecution or aggression.

Question: How would your former co-workers describe you?

Analysis: The response to this question can be very telling—more because of how the applicant reacts than how he or she answers. Does the candidate's body language stiffen or seem defensive? How do the applicant's demeanor and voice change when asked this question? With all this in mind, remember that despite all this introspection, the person whom you are interviewing may be so narcissistic or sociopathic that he or she may not recognize how people truly see him or her. Also, a true sociopath is typically unable to empathize and therefore may answer by saying things akin to "I don't know".

Job Suitability Questions

Job suitability questions are designed to determine if the person can do the job and whether or not you want them on your team. These questions are as varied as the jobs themselves and you shouldn't have any difficulty constructing these questions. Remember the liar's tells however, a desperate job seeker may well lie through his or her teeth and misrepresent their aptitude and team spirit, but by knowing their tells you will be less likely to end up with the wrong person.

Remember to ask all the candidates the SAME questions to avoid the appearance of (or even the subconscious presence of) bias. The law protects people against illegal discrimination and one of the easiest tests to PROVE illegal discrimination is to show a pattern of asking one group of people more questions, or more probing questions, or...well you get the picture.

Interestingly, I get a lot of questions from job seekers about discrimination. The hiring and screening of candidates is by its very nature is discriminatory, but not all discrimination is illegal. The Equal Opportunity Commission identifies illegal discrimination (as defined by Title VII of the Civil Rights Act of 1964 (Title VII) as using the following factors as a criteria for hiring:

- Race

- Color,

- religion,

- sex, or

- national origin;

The law also makes it illegal to retaliate against a person because the person complained about discrimination, filed a charge of discrimination, or participated in an employment discrimination investigation or lawsuit. The law also requires that employers reasonably accommodate applicants' and employees' sincerely held religious practices, unless doing so would impose an undue hardship on the operation of the employer's business. ace, color, religion, sex, or national origin;

Title VII has been amended to include the following laws:

"The Pregnancy Discrimination Act

This law amended Title VII to make it illegal to discriminate against a woman because of pregnancy, childbirth, or a medical condition related to pregnancy or childbirth. The law also makes it illegal to retaliate against a person because the person complained about discrimination, filed a charge of discrimination, or participated in an employment discrimination investigation or lawsuit.

The Equal Pay Act of 1963 (EPA)

This law makes it illegal to pay different wages to men and women if they perform equal work in the same workplace. The law also makes it illegal to retaliate against a person because the person complained about discrimination, filed a charge of discrimination, or participated in an employment discrimination investigation or lawsuit.

The Age Discrimination in Employment Act of 1967 (ADEA)

This law protects people who are 40 or older from discrimination because of age. The law also makes it illegal to retaliate against a person because the person complained about discrimination, filed a charge of discrimination, or participated in an employment discrimination investigation or lawsuit.

Title I of the Americans with Disabilities Act of 1990 (ADA)

This law makes it illegal to discriminate against a qualified person with a disability in the private sector and in state and local governments. The law also makes it illegal to retaliate against a person because the person complained about discrimination, filed a charge of discrimination, or participated in an employment discrimination investigation or lawsuit. The law also requires that employers reasonably accommodate the known physical or mental limitations of an otherwise qualified individual with a disability who is an applicant or employee, unless doing so would impose an undue hardship on the operation of the employer's business. The one

Sections 102 and 103 of the Civil Rights Act of 1991

Among other things, this law amends Title VII and the ADA to permit jury trials and compensatory and punitive damage awards in intentional discrimination cases.

Sections 501 and 505 of the Rehabilitation Act of 1973

This law makes it illegal to discriminate against a qualified person with a disability in the federal government. The law also makes it illegal to retaliate against a person because the person complained about discrimination, filed a charge of discrimination, or participated in an employment discrimination investigation or lawsuit. The law also requires that employers reasonably accommodate the known physical or mental limitations of an otherwise qualified individual with a disability who is an applicant or employee, unless doing so would impose an undue hardship on the operation of the employer's business.

The Genetic Information Nondiscrimination Act of 2008 (GINA)

Effective - November 21, 2009.

This law makes it illegal to discriminate against employees or applicants because of genetic information. Genetic information includes information about an individual's genetic tests and the genetic tests of an individual's family members, as well as information about any disease, disorder or condition of an individual's family members (i.e. an individual's family medical history). The law also makes it illegal to retaliate against a person because the person complained about discrimination, filed a charge of discrimination, or participated in an employment discrimination investigation or lawsuit."

[14]The law doesn't protect you from everything; you can be discriminated against for:

- Showing up late for an interview

- Lack of bona fide job requirements

- Unfavorable comparison to other candidates (they're just plain BETTER than you

- Your attitude during a job interview

- Not liking the musical genius Tom Waits

---

[14] *Source: https://www.eeoc.gov/laws/statutes/index.cfm*

- Acting in any way that a reasonable could assume you pose a threat to other workers or customers

- Eating chili dogs during the interview

- Getting on the nerves of the interviewer

- Looking like my 5th grade teacher, or

- behaving like a drug addled loon with the behavior and hygiene of a feral hog.

This list is far from all-inclusive and remember the whole point of the interview isn't just to find a qualified candidate but also to find a good, and safe, addition to your team.

I remember a coworker showing me the resumé of a candidate who would be working for her. I remarked that the individual had six jobs in three years, and I found that disconcerting. My coworker told me that she had the same initial response, but that she had interviewed him, and he had a good answer for his short tenure at each of his jobs. I interviewed him but caught a bad vibe from him and told her about my misgivings. He had spent several tours in the service but left abruptly one tour shy of a pension. I thought that was suspicious, or at very least showed poor judgement, but thought "who am to make (or pass) judgements on people's life choices?"

When I voiced my concerns to my coworker, she dismissed them and accused me of not wanting to hire another man who would "challenge (my) alpha dog status". I found the accusation insulting and told her so, but added, "hey, he will be your employee so if it goes south it's your problem."

Soon the president of the company came to me and asked me to come to his office to talk. He told me that hiring this man shouldn't be perceived as a threat to me and that I will always have a position of leadership and expertise in the organization. I explained to him that I was asked my opinion and gave it. I didn't feel threatened but 1) he was far from 100% qualified to do the job 2) he would require extensive training that would fall to me and I wasn't sure how well that would sit with him and 3) his job history over the past 2 years showed that he had and average tenure of 3 months on the job, and had gaps between each indicating, to me at least, a strong possibility of abrupt dismissals and or quitting.

They hired him, and he was almost immediately a problem. I don't remember what set him off but he came into my office shouting at me about some perceived grievance and he even hinted that he might be provoked into violence. I went to his manager and to the president of the company and reported the incident and, predictably, they did nothing except dismiss my complaints by saying "you're just looking to find fault" and "you never liked him and nothing he does will ever please you."

Over the next couple of months there were other indicators that this man was a hot head and potentially unstable. He complained bitterly about his neighbors with whom he was feuding (not A neighbor but multiple neighbors. I knew how his manager and the president would respond to my concerns, so I said nothing.

On several occasions this guy would go off his nut and send me long rambling emails containing threats both veiled and overt. In one, a 5-page email, he told me that we could handle this in two ways "hard or easy". In each case, I printed out the emails and put them in a file.

One day his manager came to me looking stricken. She had received an email from him that was tame in comparison made to the ones he made to me. I merely pulled out the file and handed it to him. She pulled me into an impromptu meeting with the president, where I was asked why I had not come forward with my emails sooner and I told them flat out because:

A) I don't believe they wouldn't believe me and

B) I believed they would take no action.

The individual was fired soon after the meeting.

At this point his manager was terrified that he would come and shoot up the office and the company took appropriate measures to protect the premises. "But what about the parking lot? His manager asked me, and I didn't have an answer. Fortunately, he never returned, and we never heard from him again, but it is safe to say that it wouldn't take many other variables to have this become a workplace violence event and one that could have been readily prevented.

Here is an example where listening to one's gut, and not ignoring red flags resulted in a bad hire, and too often Human Resources, desperate to find a body, allows this to happens.

It's fine to talk about avoiding bad hires, we all try to do that anyway, and we can't screen out everyone who may be capable of homicide (under the right circumstances just about anyone is capable of committing a homicide or being the target of a violent act.) or someone who is likely to be a target, but what about the people you have on staff who are already exhibiting instability, or those who were once model workers and now are exhibiting violent tendencies or acting unstable?

Many will tell you to immediately engage your disciplinary process and begin the process of weeding the person out; this is one of the best ways to trigger an event. No matter whether the person is a target or a potential triggerman follow these basic steps:

1. **Be alert,** in the next chapter we will talk about how to spot the warning signs, so I won't rehash them here, but the moment you finish reading chapter 4, I want you to put down the book and really think about your workforce in the context of these warning signs.

2. **Know the triggers,** Divorce and/or infidelity (real or imagined) are triggers for violence against women, and firing or the threat of firing is generally a trigger for

78

single shooter event where the boss is the primary target. So, act early and intervene, not as a heavy-handed disciplinarian, but as a genuinely caring coach. In the case of a divorce/separation you can sit down with the affected party and ask how their ex-spouse/partner/romantic entanglement is handling the situation? Ask the person if their domestic partner has access to firearms and if he or she has ever become violent, if he or she thinks extra protection is warranted. You can also ask if he or she has a protective order in place or needs help getting one (a lot of people don't know where to start). Reassure the person that you are on his or her side and you will do your utmost to protect him or her.

In the case of the person in a downward spiral, once again, intervene EARLY. Offer help, and make it clear that you are an advocate for him or her. Again, take great pains to convince them that you are on his or her side and you want them to succeed. There is typically a long road between poor performance and firing, and it is seldom a single event that results in a firing. Showing some genuine interest in salvaging a person's career can go a long way to preventing violence. More often than not, the single shooter believes he has been unfairly treated and feels he has been persecuted.

I once worked at a firm where one socially maladroit manager caught one of his workers who was very far behind in his work, playing solitaire on his computer instead of working. He blew up and fired him immediately against all Human Resource policy. The worker had to be reinstated to avoid legal difficulties, and something had to be done with the manager. He was sent to me, (part of my duties was to coach those on performance improvement plans) and I am proud to say that after some coaching and training he became a very successful member of the leadership team.

Knowing him as I do, he most certainly lost his cool but was not a likely candidate for becoming a single shooter, BUT, had the company done nothing in response to this it would likely embolden others to behave inappropriately.

3. **Take action.** Worrying doesn't prevent violent outbursts or thwart attacks, taking action does. Taking action can be as simple is reporting the abhorrent behavior to a supervisor or filing a formal complaint with Human Resources. A common reason for inaction is "I don't want him coming after me" and this excuse gets people killed.

4. **Involve law enforcement of a credible threat early.** You don't be need to run to the cops like chicken little at the first sign of potential problem, but on the other hand if an Employee firing turns particularity ugly notifying law enforcement of the situation is a prudent move.

5. **Alert your workforce of the threat.** Alerting your workers of a potential threat is a tightrope. You want to alert them of the potential threat without causing a panic or providing the potential attacker's grounds for a lawsuit.

   • **Make sure you emphasize that this is only a *potential threat.*** There is a massive difference between a potential threat and an actual threat. While heightened vigilance is certainly in order you don't need to create a panic.

   • **Stick to the facts they NEED.** People don't need to know all the sordid details of a co-worker's life but facts like it is a domestic dispute, a credible threat, the individual is likely armed, and people should notify Human Resources immediately if they see something suspicious and to call 911 (or

80

9911 if your phone system requires you to dial a 9
for an outside line) if they see an imminent threat.

- **Emphasize that as long as the threat exists there
  will be no drills.** Some people are more than a little
  nonchalant when it comes to drills and may ignore
  an actual alarm because they believe it is a drill.

- **Reinforce security procedures.** This is an
  excellent time to remind you staff that things like
  holding a coded door or elevator for someone else-
  -even a known coworker are dangerous and
  prohibited.

Dealing with Problem Employees After the Hire

Much as we try to avoid hiring a potentially dangerous person
or unwittingly hire a potential target, sometimes we fail and
have to deal with a person who we now realize we should never
have hired. There are some easy ways to handle this:

- **Deal with the problem early.** When I hire someone, I
  am sometimes alarmed at their failure to exhibit "new

hire behaviors". These behaviors can range from overly familiar conversations to downright belligerent behavior. Sometimes this behavior is simply because of a lack of experience in the workplace. In other cases, it's because the person desperately wants to conform and are trying too hard. Whatever the case intercede early and provide feedback on the person's performance and your expectations.

- **Don't make excuses for the person.** Making excuses for a person is just a way to avoid conflict. If the person is sending off red flags than you should deal with them immediately.

I once worked in an office where a fresh grad was hired (at a much higher rate than the rest of the people who had more experience and at least as much education). On his second day he told me my music was horrible (I will put up with a lot, but when you mock Tom Waits, you better be prepared to defend yourself verbally, of course). On day two he drove a bunch of us to lunch, where a female coworker found a pornographic magazine in the backseat of his car, and over lunch he admitted that he had lied during his job interview, oh I forgot to mention that his boss was at the lunch. But the boss made excuses—"he was new", "he didn't have a lot of "office" experience", "he would learn appropriate behavior", "he was just trying to fit in."

His goose finally cooked when he was fired after he played a practical joke with anti-semitic overtones.

- **Exercise the Probationary/At-Will Dismissal Option.** If you really think that the person is beyond coaching (and you're company is, like most, an "at-will" employer) you can dismiss someone during his or her probationary period without any cause or explanation. Similarly, if you are an at-will employer you don't need a reason to dismiss someone (nor do they need to provide you with notice or a reason for quitting.)

- **Reinforce your expectations of their behavior.** When it comes to changing behaviors, repetition is the key. Having a serious dialog about the gaps in the employee's behavior and your expectations. If the behavior continues, have another talk but this time make sure your message is clear by having them repeat back to you your expectations of his or her behavior and the gaps between it and your expectations.

Providing Feedback

People are forever providing us with information about our behavior, this practice is called feedback. Ideally, feedback is given to us to help us to improve our relationships, but as often as not, feedback is provided to make the speaker feel better without regard to whether or not the feedback is accurate, welcome, or in any way useful. If we are providing feedback to a worker whose behavior, we want to change it's essential that we provide feedback appropriately.

Before providing feedback, we need to recognize that there are right ways and wrong ways of giving information regarding behavior to someone else. The first rule of providing feedback is to focus on behaviors, not attitudes. Unfortunately, many people are seemingly unable to make the distinction between who we are as people and how we behave. Contrary to what many believe, we cannot control our emotions.

We feel what we feel because of chemical electric signals that run through our brain. If the stimuli that our nervous system picks up are such that the brain tells us to be angry, we will be angry. If it says we should be happy whether it seems logical to feel that way or not, we are happy. Barring chemical

83

imbalances, psychological illness, or a malfunction of the brain, this is how life works.

That is not to say that we are hapless victims of our internal chemical plant. While we may not be able to control our emotions—how we feel—we can certainly control our behaviors—how we act on what we feel. Oft-times people provide us feedback on our emotions instead of on our behavior. The result of this muddied feedback is that often-times people say things like "you have a shit attitude" rather than "I find it upsetting when you use that tone of voice when speaking to me." The first statement is unproductive and stress producing for a variety of reasons and if you are dealing with someone capable of violence you have initiated the process of provoking it. Some of the more faint of heart may take umbrage at my scatological language, but trust me it is warranted.

The first statement attacks the essence of who we are as human beings. After all, where do attitudes come from? What people frequently describe as an attitude is the physical manifestation of our emotions. And where do our emotions come from? Emotions—though many are loath to admit it—are created by chemicals in our brain. Where do the chemicals in our brain come from? Our brains produce these chemicals—completely involuntarily—in response to external stimuli.

So, when someone tells you that you have a shit attitude, they are essentially saying that your emotions are shit, and (continuing the logic stream) that you have shit in your brain. This feedback isn't exactly the kind of "up with people" sentiment that is likely to put one at ease, rather it elicits a "circle the wagons" response that churns out more chemicals and heightens our stress level. It most certainly doesn't help the worker to become more resilience.

Types of Feedback

There are four basic kinds of feedback (Silence, Criticism,

Advice, and Reinforcement) and each has an inappropriate and an inappropriate circumstance in which it should be used.

Silence

Perhaps the most common form of feedback is silence. Silence could also be described as the absence of feedback when feedback is expected. Silence is appropriate for the times in life where we want everything to stay the same. "If you weren't happy, why didn't you say something?" Silence is often an excellent tool for remaining cool when your emotions are raging, but silence is a short-term fix.

Often, we use silence as a flight mechanism, we don't want to fight, so we mentally extricate ourselves from the situation by remaining silent, rather than providing more direct feedback and potentially provoking further attack, we remain silent and let things simmer. Silence should be used sparingly; it hurts relationships as we ascribe sinister motives to the person from whom we receive no information. As our brains have only partial information with which to determine whether or not we are in danger we react as if the silent ones are hostile to us. Many an employee inaccurately assumes that his or her boss doesn't like him or her simply because the employer has not provided enough reassurance to the contrary.

Years ago, I had a job that required a heavy travel schedule, which in turn meant that I had very little contact with my boss. Soon I became convinced that my boss was out to get me, and that—despite constant praise from my customers, and positive performance reviews—I was in imminent danger of being fired. It is interesting to note, that even though I was fully aware that my paranoia was a direct result of a lack of feedback from my boss, I was unable to shake my raging paranoia; my subconscious was far stronger than my intellect. (Not something of which I am especially proud; let's just say I don't have it on my resume.)

Criticism

Another form of feedback is criticism. Criticism is the practice of sharing negative information about us without any other information. Criticism is essentially an attack—someone tells us that what we are doing is bad, wrong, or otherwise undesirable.

Repeated criticism hurts relationship; a big surprise—we tend to dislike people who continually remind us of how stupid we are, how much we need to improve, or how foolish we've acted. As we are in close proximity with people who criticize us, we are increasingly likely to employ a fight/flight response. If we spend enough time with the person and our fight response is engaged, it is highly likely that we will lash out at that person either overtly or covertly.

An overt aggressive response can take the form of a verbal blow up or in extreme cases physical violence. Take for example the case of the worker who is continually criticized by his boss. Day after day the boss knit picks about the quality of the work. One day the criticism becomes too much and the employee explodes in a flurry of obscenity, he tells the boss in dubious anatomical accuracy specifically in which orifices the boss can stick this month's status reports. Add to this, mental illness and alcohol and you may likely have a single-shooter event that not only could you have prevented, but that you actually caused, or at the very least facilitated.

The aggression is far more likely to be covert. In the previous example the employee became overtly hostile as his fight/flight lever got switched to fight. In a far more likely scenario, the employee becomes passive aggressive. Instead of obscenity and creative anatomical body packing the injured employee takes the fight underground. Graffiti gets sprawled on bathroom walls; deadlines get "innocently" missed; key information is not conveyed, and the employee engages in malicious obedience. Passive aggression doesn't relieve stress, however, and in many cases leads to guilt as our stress level subsides.

Sometimes criticism triggers the flight response; instead of fighting we flee. The flight response manifests itself in a phenomenon called escape and avoidance. In other words, we—often without realizing it—will quickly excuse ourselves from the company of the person who over-criticizes us (escape) or, when we are able, avoid contact with the criticizer altogether.

My ex-wife and I used to like to play a little game we called "what's wrong with Phil". The game begins with her saying, "you know what's wrong with you?" As much as I love this game (I actually lettered in it in high school.) I find myself saying, "You know how much I love this game, and how I thirst for information to help me on my road to self-discovery and ultimate self-actualization, however, I have pressing business elsewhere."

It comes as no surprise that I don't want to listen to an attack on who I am as a person, but any response short of fleeing the scene is likely to provoke more, and escalated criticism.

Sometimes the criticism is subtle, the person providing feedback isn't directly telling you that you're broken, they insinuate that you're broken: "You should buy a house; renting is for suckers." "You should sell real estate: there's good money in it." Did you ever notice how some people can make you feel like crap while sounding so very helpful?

It's irritating and yet we feel guilty for being irritated since they were "only trying to help." The instances where people offer us help when we've never as much as hinted that we needed assistance is maddening. Why does it irritate us? They're just trying to help out, right? When someone tells us that "we should..."it is an act of aggression. Once again or flight and fight goes on alert, our brains flood our bodies with chemicals, and our bodies brace themselves for a fight. Sometimes we respond with, "you should shut the hell up and mind your own business (fight) or "yeah, you're right" (flight.) When it comes to some people, they will "should" all over us if we let them. Don't let people:"should" all over you.

However well intentioned, the people who provide us with unsolicited criticism cause us stress. The unspoken message in the "you should…" is that if you continuing doing what you are doing you are broken in some way. The more passive their aggression the more alert our bodies become and the more stress-related problems we suffer as a result.

Criticism tends to eliminate related behaviors that we value. For example, let's say you are the first to arrive at the office every day and the task of making the coffee falls to you. You don't mind, you do it because you like drinking coffee, it's not hard to do, and you like helping out the group. Now, one day, I come up to you and say, "you know, I'm getting sick of having to put away the coffee filters, mopping up the little puddles you leave behind, and sweeping up coffee grounds. You'd think at your age you'd have learned to clean up after yourself." After my reproach of your coffee making, what are the chances that you will be making any coffee (safe for me to drink) anytime soon? Chances are great that you will either stop making coffee (flight), tell me that I can make the coffee from now on (fight), or continue making coffee but now deliberately leaving a bigger mess (passive aggressive). In all these cases, our goal to get me to pick up after myself are left un-achieved, and in two thirds of the cases a highly desirable behavior falls along the wayside. Clearly, a feedback tool that does not trigger the fight/flight response is necessary.

Not all feedback is dysfunctional, in fact, good, constructive feedback is essential for lowering our stress.

Advice

A far more effective feedback mechanism is advice. Where criticism is destructive and focuses on negative aspects, advice is the practice of providing a more balanced description of the behavior. When providing advice, we begin by discussing positive behaviors before discussing behaviors we would like to see changed. Our example of the coffee-making mess could have been handled using advice instead of criticism and would likely have a much more positive result.

Instead of complaining about the negative aspects of the coffee I should have started by commenting on the things in your behavior that I valued before moving on to the behaviors I would like to see changed. "I want you to know that I love it that you make coffee every day; I am NOT a morning person and I rely on that first cup of coffee. I also need your help. Often, the kitchen area is a mess, in a large part because of the coffee that you make. How can I help you to clean up after yourself?"

I can already hear some of you laughing, "yeah right...they'll just say 'you clean it if it bothers you'"...maybe, and if you lack that person's trust probably; if you have an ulterior motive; definitely. If you are insincere in your praise, you create, what a friend of mine indelicately dubbed, the shit-filled twinkie. The shit-filled twinkie is a comment that at first appears to be a compliment (a delicious-looking snack cake), but inside the compliment is an insult (need I further explain the analogy?) In the interest of decorum, let's refer to my friend's analogy as the SFT. SFTs are created because the speaker is just going through the motions of commenting on positive elements of the behavior. SFTs do more harm than good.

Far from being a SFT, this approach mends troubled relationships and helps to build trust. As you build trust, your stress level, and the stress level of the other person diminishes. Remember though, building trust takes time. Initially, the person receiving the feedback is likely to resist this change in you and only through patient, consistent advice will the relationship ultimately be mended.

I realized that I was overusing advice one day when after praising one of my staff members she said "but..." I felt awful, here I was trying to really to compliment her, but I had overused advice so much she was leery of my comments.

Reinforcement

Another outstanding way to provide feedback is through reinforcement. Reinforcement is used to increase desired behaviors. Basically, reinforcement is a sincere, meaningful compliment. It is a way of thanking people for doing things right and letting them know they appreciate what they've done for us. The danger of over using reinforcement is that you may inadvertently strengthen related undesirable behaviors as well.

Silence	Criticism
Appropriate Use: When emotions are running hot **Overuse Leads To:** Paranoia, damaged relationship.	**Appropriate Use**: When there are no associated positive behaviors **Overuse Leads To:** Escape and avoidance, damaged relationships, outburst of aggression or violence
Advice	Reinforcement
Appropriate Use: When the other person is primarily a good person but has a bad habit or two **Overuse Leads To:** SFT (let's not go back there)	**Appropriate Use**: When the other person has done an outstanding job and there is no unwanted behavior associated **Overuse Leads To:** the feeling that you are being insincere or condescending.

Rules for Providing Feedback

Effective feedback generally follows these basic rules:

1. **Be timely.** Nothing demoralizes me more than my performance evaluation. Not because it's one-way (I never get to tell my boss to evaluate himself and then regurgitate back to him as if I had thought of it) no, it's because it happens once a year. It bothered you that I was late last February? Well then why didn't you say something than you malicious little pustule? Any other nits you've been waiting to pick. For the record my boss isn't like that, but I have had some who were. Timely feedback has a greater impact on us and we are more likely to internalize it and act on the feedback in a positive way.

2. **Be specific.** Anytime you tell a worker that people are saying this or that you the immediate response is "who is saying that?" It's only natural to challenge what someone has HEARD about you. Providing specific examples of what YOU have observed and how YOU feel about what you have observed is powerful; non-specific feedback is non-actionable garbage.

3. **Ask permission to provide feedback.** Just because you have the authority to tell me how I should behave doesn't mean that I am always in the right frame of mind to hear what you want to say to me. Always begin a feedback session

4. **Use "I" statements.** I statements are observations given from the first person. I saw, I don't like, I think, are all "I" statements. I statements make it difficult to dismiss the feedback as unfounded or hearsay. I statements also allow the recipient of the feedback to ask for clarification or for more specifics.

5. **Focus on behaviors.** I can't control how I feel, but I can control how I act on those feelings. No one has the right to tell another person how that other person should or should not feel, but you are completely within your rights in telling me your expectations of my behavior.

6. **Don't assume you know my motivation.** It's too easy to try to soften the blow by making excuses for my behavior. Saying, "I know you were frustrated BUT" or something similar dilutes the feedback and make you look soft and cowardly.

7. **Provide feedback privately.** Sometimes providing feedback publicly can provoke an unstable individual into violence. Feedback is an intimate act and like all acts of intimacy should be kept private. Embarrassing an unstable individual by publicly airing your grievances could be the trigger that sets a violent rampage into action—even if it takes months to manifest.

8. **Focus on the Other Person's Growth.** If you just want to complain about how a person has behaved, that's not really giving feedback. Feedback should contain three main elements: A behavior that you have observed and appreciate, something you value in the other person's behaviors and advice as to how they might be even more effective. I used to work at a company that had a short, standard way to give feedback. "I think you do an excellent job at _____, and I value your_____ and I think you will be even more effective if you _____."
    At first giving feedback in this way made me feel like a soft-head sap, but eventually I found that the standard format made it easier to put aside my emotions and give honest feedback.

9. **Thank the person to whom you have given feedback.** Thanking the person to whom you just provided feedback makes you both feel better. Let's face it, it's not always easy to give (or receive) feedback and sincerely thanking the person for taking the time to listen and showing you the courtesy of not blowing up, making excuses, or otherwise being a

 *Lone Gunman*

loathsome toad recognizes and acknowledges his or her
generous cooperation

Chapter 4: Spotting the Warning Signs

Single shooter events are the last-ditch attempt to create change; it is the act of someone who is typically very controlling and who feels that he or she is out of options. His or her life is likely spiraling out of control. The single shooter in the workplace is trying to exert the control he or she feels he or she has lost. Workplace violence is also typically carried out with by individuals who are heavy alcohol or drug users (at least at the time of the attack—they may have been teetotalers before their lives took an ugly turn).

These individuals have been given every chance and typically are out of any sort of options. They carry a grudge for an injustice—real or imagined—and feel like they have no other alternative; they are cashing in their proverbial chips and going out in a blaze of glory and gore. Workplace violence is typically not motivated by hate, rather they are motivated by desperation, defeat and fueled by alcohol. Single shooter workplace events are the one last act to demonstrate that the shooter still has some modicum of control over his or her life and the lives of his victims.

Workplace violence seldom erupts without a string of warning signs—typically a small and seemingly petty or insignificant event like an insult or inappropriate behavior—and you and your organization's ability to spot the warning signs of a troubled employee or a potential target can mean the difference literally between life and a death. Treating any worker grievance—no matter how small or insignificant—seriously can literally be a matter of life and death.

Obviously, it's easier to deal with a tense a situation using de-escalation techniques but the secret to the success of these techniques is getting involved early; ignoring these warning signs can result in a situation that is much more difficult to deal with later.

What employees are most likely to become unhinged?

Of course, there are no perfect predictors of a workplace lone gunman, and as I have stated at length, you shouldn't jump to any rash judgments about an individual just because of a couple of suspicious or odd behaviors. That having been said, some of the warning signs that an individual is becoming unstable (and these warning signs can apply to both perpetrators and targets) include:

- Behavioral changes

    o **A marked change in personality.** One of the first and most notable changes that something is amiss in a person's life is a sudden and marked change in attitude. Someone suffering from outside stimuli that could trigger a violent episode often exhibit paradoxical changes in their behavior, particularly from friendly and sociable to sullen and antisocial, or from quiet and reserved to loud and bold.

This change in behavior can also indicate drug use, which in itself is also an indicator. On the other hand, someone who is a potential target for violence may become withdrawn, quiet, and antisocial.

o **Lethargy or apathy.** When a person feels that they are running out of options, this feeling of malaise can manifest in lethargy or apathy. The individual stops caring about the consequences of his or her actions and the day-to-day mundanity of the job. This can apply to either the perpetrator or the target as both are in a horrible environment from which they can see no way out.

o **Becoming overly and inappropriately emotional.** What, you may ask, constitutes "inappropriate" behavior or becoming "overly emotional"? Crying over the loss of a parent is appropriately emotional, crying over the loss of a blue pen is not. To some extent overly emotional is in the eye of the beholder. But when you view the behavior through the lens of workplace violence you need to concentrate on dramatic changes in behavior and subtle shifts.

Often the feelings of hopelessness and loss of control that precede a single shooter event, result in emotional outbursts that are out of character particularly angry outbursts, crying jags, or pouting.

o **Joking about or threatening violence.** Joking about violence means that consciously or unconsciously the person telling the joke is

97

thinking about violence. Thinking about violence is not the same as planning violence, but it is another checkmark on our list of indicators of workplace violence. Threatening violence, even in a non-threatening tone, is far more serious and should be dealt with swiftly and decisively. These threats can be spoken or made through emails, in conversation, or subtle innuendo.

I used to work with two men who both talked a lot about violence. One, a jovial coworker whose sense of humor held nothing sacred, openly speculated about his "kill route"; he wasn't serious, and we all knew it, but in retrospect, it probably was unwise for his coworkers and boss to ignore the gallows humor. The other coworker was a kind and introverted man. He would often tell me, "one of these days I'm going to come in and kill all of you" to which I would reply, "now I want you to remember two things, 1) I have always been nice to you and 2) I am out on Tuesdays; I'll leave a list".

Could I have handled it better? Certainly, but then I was young, and this was before shooting up the office was seemingly as common as quitting without notice. Neither threat was serious, credible, or alarming, and I think they illustrate nicely that someone who jokes about violence more often than not is not someone who will commit the acts about which he jokes, but then again, they should be considered another red flag.

- o **Persecution complexes and delusional thoughts.** A worker who fails to acknowledge

98

his or her drop in performance, and blames others or claims that everyone is out to get them may be prone to violence—although generally speaking this is just a personality type and it's important to recognize that a possibility of violent behavior is not the same as a propensity for violent behavior which is not the same as a predictor of violent behavior.

These people will blame others for their mistakes and make repeated excuses. They may accuse their superiors of playing favorites or being "out to get them". They will tend to look for reasons to take offense and will often take things very personally. These people will deflect criticism by claiming that "everyone" is doing it and may actually believe that they are being singled out for punishment.

I once worked with a man who blew up and called a particularly loathsome customer a series of obscenities many of which I am still looking up. The customer was predictably upset and called the president of the company. After conferring with the lawyers, they decided that this co-worker needed to be fired. (Yes, I know the absurdity of feeling as though you have to check with the lawyers before firing someone who did something like this.) The confab took about three days, in which this dysfunctional imbecile committed THREE additional fireable offenses including a complaint of sexual harassment!

He was by all accounts a creepy little man who often expressed feelings of persecution, and jealousy (he felt others were jealous of his work—truthfully, I admit envying his

only did he create an uncomfortable work environment, but he made us all feel unsafe as he turned up the pressure on coworkers who we already considered dangerous.

When I tell some men that I worked for a woman, many of them are incredulous and openly say, "I could NEVER work for a woman!" I never understood this misogyny, and would usually deflect it by saying, "my mom was a woman and I have four older sisters, so I am used to being bossed around by women. Frankly, getting paid for it is a nice change." Most women hating men are savvy enough to keep their opinions to themselves, but they're still out there and they are potentially dangerous.

- Physical changes

  o **Poor hygiene, wearing dirty clothing.** It's one thing if someone has body odor from the day you hired them (and why for the love of all that's holy did you higher stinky?) and quite another if the body odor develops suddenly and is in conjunction with other physical changes.

  Tread lightly here. You are within your rights to confront a worker about poor hygiene, but you cannot pry about physical conditions that might be causing said odors. Here again, there is a gulf of difference between Jimmy in the mailroom who likes to skip his morning shower and throw on yesterday's shirt, so he can get an extra 10 minutes of sleep, and Joe the normally fastidiously dressed salesman who starts coming in one day looking like a mud wrestler and smelling like a honey dipper. In both

102

cases, friendly, non-adversarial coaching is appropriate.

o **Bruising, cuts, or other indications of fighting.** While the first rule of "Fight Club is you don't talk about Fight Club", you're not IN fight club, you are in a position of authority and you have a responsibility to talk about what physical changes you have observed. Be sure that you don't interrogate the worker but express in compassionate terms your concern for their well-being. Indications of fighting can be indicative of either an abuser or an abused worker and in either case it should not be ignored.

o **Watery eyes and blotchy skin.** Watery eyes and blotchy skin can indicate a change in diet, physical illness or abuse, or drug/alcohol abuse. Together with these other indicators, they can add up to an unstable individual, or simply an insomniac. Either way, there is nothing wrong with a show of genuine concern, like asking, "do you feel okay?"

o **Complaints about a vague feeling of illness or tiredness.** High levels of stress can manifest as vague aches and pains, lack of energy, or other vague illnesses. Too often in our society, we dismiss an overly stressed worker as a hypochondriac or a crybaby. These symptoms are not imaginary and acting in a way that tells the worker that you don't sympathize can be another paving stone in the road to an explosion. Also, a victim of domestic violence may exhibit these same symptoms. Intervening early can save lives.

Perhaps most important is to encourage everyone in the organization that if they see something suspicious, to say something to a person in authority, and do something like getting to safety or monitoring the situation until help arrives.

Chapter 5: What work environments can trigger an event?

I have worked in my fair share of toxic work environments, and in at least four of them there has been a workplace homicide (two of the shootings occurred after I no longer worked at the companies and in two cases the murder victims were ambushed off site.) In all the cases that happened in workplaces I worked or had worked the motive was all the same: a lover's triangle.

Extramarital affairs tend to be a strong and extremely common cause of workplace violence. My own marriage broke up as a result of my ex-wife cheating on me with at least one co-worker, I can tell you first hand that such an experience isn't any kind of fun, if fact it's as close to Hell as I ever want to come. But that was over 25 years ago and in deference to my daughters' privacy I will spare you the gory details of the rest of her life that ended abruptly 2 years ago. Karma always seems to exact a horrible price.

I'm told that good living is the best revenge—personally I've always thought that throwing acid in someone's face is the best revenge, but practically speaking I don't know where to get acid and can say with some surety that I would likely as not spill it on myself, so a lack of ambition and an abundance of pragmatism stopped me from attempting to exact any revenge besides enjoying time with my daughters, doing what the hell I want when I want, and making (and spending) a boatload of money. In this chapter I will deal with two types of toxic cultures: the dating game culture, and the tyrant's rule culture.

The dating game culture

There is a strange dichotomy in the law regarding dating in the workplace. On one hand courts have upheld a company's employees' right to date one another (although to call these rulings murky is to do mud an injustice) and on the other hand, workplace romances gone wrong is one of the most common causes of workplace violence, especially if the woman (almost exclusively) is married or divorcing her spouse.

The wronged husband or cheated on boyfriend, whose life is spiraling out of control, gets a couple of drinks in him loads up the gun and heads to the one place his intended targets will be: at work. The shooter tends to kill the woman, her current paramour, and the boss for good measure (typically, the shooter has a less than amicable opinion of bosses in general and what the hell he bought six bullets…) Good samaritans often get caught in the crossfire and the gunmen, in a final act of complete control commits suicide.

So, what can you do to prevent this? Focus exclusively on work performance. I have yet to see a workplace romance that wasn't widely known and disruptive. I worked at one company where one department had more sexual activity going on than the court of Caligula.

Eunuch managers whine that "there's nothing I can do…we don't have a policy" to which I would always reply (and forgive my crude language, but if you are that sensitive seriously why are your reading this?) "we don't have a policy against me shitting in your waste basket, but if I kept doing it you would find a way to get me to stop." We'll cover more about policies that you can enact in a later chapter but in general, you can shut down the dating game culture by focusing on tangentially related behaviors where the dating of coworkers becomes problematic not because they're dating but because they are acting like imbeciles. I know of one case where a married executive was having an affair with his married secretary.

The murky waters around the legality of disciplining employees from dating caused the legal council to get creative. Eventually, both were fired for cause…for misuse of office equipment. I wish this anecdote was a lot more juicy than it is, but the fact is the two were engaging in obscene phone calls with one another using their company phones.

The policy on phone usage was clear: your business telephone was for the exclusive use of business purposes and any other such use was considered a misuse of office equipment which was a fireable offense. This was an extreme case and it probably had more to do with avoiding a large severance package (fired for cause meant the offending party forfeited the right to a severance package) than the dating but dating in the workplace opens up a pandora's box of workplace risks from sexual harassment to workplace violence so it cannot be ignored and must be managed carefully.

I used to supervise a young, friendly, upbeat, woman just starting her career. A day didn't go by where men contrived reasons to talk to her. Although she did nothing to knowingly encourage them (she was fairly naive) the whole scene reminded me of when my childhood dog went into heat and dogs who, let's face is—she was so far out of their leagues that they didn't have a chance—came from all over the county to pitch their woo.

I sat her down and talked to her. I explained that she had done nothing wrong, BUT her gentlemen callers were preventing HER from getting her work done and preventing THEM from getting their work done. I further explained that if she wished to see any of them socially, she should accept invitations for lunch, but she needed to let them know that apart from her lunch break she was not interested in having them visit her in her work area.

This cleared the issue up nicely. I dealt with work and performance issues and only those. If she didn't like it, she never said anything about it, and frankly, it didn't matter, she was not paid to flirt, and her erstwhile gentlemen callers weren't being paid to walk around like lotharios walking around the hotel bar at happy hour.

The tyrant culture

Unfortunately, I have worked in more than one Tyrant Culture. Most of you can probably relate to the bully-boy boss who gets his (or her) jollies from sending people fleeing his (or her) office in terror. Conventional wisdom holds that bullies, deep down, are cowards, and all you need to do is to stand up to them. I found that this is great advice for getting the snot knocked out of you.

Bullies, contrary to popular belief aren't stupid, well at least not stupid enough to pick on someone who has a fighting chance of winning a fight or even inflicting serious harm. It's bad when it's on the schoolyard playground (my grade school playground was a blacktop parking lot with no playground equipment surrounded by a 10-foot chain link fence complete with barbed wire atop. It was as close to the prison yard as I care to get (seriously all that was missing was ethnic gangs and an area for weight lifting and they could move the convicts in tomorrow.) But as bad as that was, it's worse when the bully has an economic power over you.

For some of us it's easy; you just quit. Or you do like I do. Years ago, I had a customer off his nut and in full on bullying mode. He was frothing at the mouth and screaming at me for doing exactly what he had asked me to do and doing it well quite frankly. Simply sat back and gave him a sublime Mona Lisa smile. After the meeting my boss was outraged, he swore that he was going to march into this man's boss's office and demand some vague form of justice.

Then he got a good look at me, smiling like Johnny Depp portraying Ed Wood. The grin of a simpleton with knowledge no one else has. "Why aren't you angry?" my boss demanded. I said, "Simple. I realize that he has all the power now, but someday, maybe quite soon, he'll just be a guy. He won't have an economic power over me. We'll just be two guys. Maybe I'll be driving through a shopping center parking lot and maybe he'll be pushing a card down the aisle. He'll look up and he'll see me, and the diabolical look on my face as I bear down on him. And in that instant, he'll know true fear." Most of us have these fantasies and that is why I will never win the lottery—too many revenge fantasies. But that's all they are, fantasies, I will never act on them and hopefully, none of you reading this will either.

Sometimes it's healthy to blow of some imaginary steam, whether it's pretending the box you are punching to break it down for recycling is your bosses head or playing a violent video game. You and I know the difference between fake violence and actual violence, but for the workplace gunman these aren't fantasies, they are, if not plans, then thumbnail sketches of what he will do to this tyrant once the bully pushes things too far.

Obviously, he knows he won't be able to drag the red-faced, fat-assed CEO dictator into the pit he dug in his basement and force "it to rub the lotion on its skin or it gets the hose again."

but he knows that he has a gun and a singularity of purpose of that one last great act of defiance.

Another Tyrant boss who I still refer to as The Devil was an ex-career military officer who demanded that his (usually imbecilic) commands were carried out without deviation or argument. So I would follow his orders knowing full well that he either lacked a key bit of information or that his idea would backfire with disastrous results. One day he called me into his office and sat me down.

He accused me of "malicious obedience" and he explained that I was guilty of subverting the spirit of his "instructions" by carrying them out as directed. I responded by saying that I routinely did as he described and would continue to do so as long as he refused to listen to my protestations. I explained that when I resisted his commands it wasn't because I was lazy, defiant, or (heaven help me) challenging his authority, but trying to warn him of the logical consequences of his own stupidity (I cleaned that last part up).

The abuse didn't come from The Devil alone, through his example, he made violence against coworkers acceptable, even encouraged. I remember on instance when during a meeting, I kept asking a coworker whose first language was not English to repeat himself. He was far behind on his project and the continued berating by the Devil made his already fairly thick accent even more difficult to understand.

For the record I was not mocking him, bullying or berating him in anyway, I simply could NOT understand what he was saying and needed the information to do my job. The meeting was tense, and he was noticeably frustrated. When the meeting broke up casually said, "you know, someday someone's going to beat the crap out of you for your smart mouth". In an offhand response, I said, "well not today". This enraged him and as soon as I turned my back, he jumped on me and punched me screaming, "don't be so sure!" Fortunately for me, the bulk of the meeting attendees, mostly men, subdued him throwing him to the ground and holding him until he got his temper under control.

Keep in mind, this gentleman criminally battered me without any deliberate or serious provocation in front of The Devil who did and said nothing. There were no work consequences—soon after he apologized, and I told him that I was not trying to embarrass him but couldn't understand him. He asked if I was going to file charges, and I said that I wouldn't THIS time, but that he should not mistake mercy for weakness.

A few weeks later, he blew up at another coworker who fled the office before there was any violence. The violent offender, sure that the other employee would insist he be dismissed went in and told The Devil off and quit. I steered clear of the office for a week or so to be sure he wasn't coming back. Shortly before I left the company, an apparently random shooter fired two shots into The Devil's moving vehicle. No one was harmed, but it was enough to shock him into somewhat less tyrannical behavior (for the record I have an alibi.)

I was never completely convinced that he was shot at, but two windows were shattered as he drove and what's more important is that HE believed an attempt had been made. As the small company he founded disintegrated he was legitimately surprised that the people he had routinely mistreated left the companies either taking key clients with them or joining the client organizations and devoting their lives to ensuring that the client never did business with him again.

Unfortunately, too often the proverbial straw that breaks the camel's back doesn't come from the tyrant, rather it is the bearer of bad news. The pallid supervisor who delivers the bad news that vacations have all been put on hold, or that raises, and bonuses will be delayed by six months or whatever triggers the gunman into doing something egregious enough to get fired.

I know one executive who openly bragged that he would fire the people who performed in lowest ten percent of the company and he ran irrespective as to whether they met their goals or not. He is a bully and proud of it. He drives people from the company he ran, but for whatever reason (one can only assume blackmail) he has kept his job.

The executive bully makes the decisions that are carried out by others who are then put at risk because typically the bully is so insulated from the unstable person that he or she doesn't recognize the danger in which he or she places the rank and file, and if he or she did the executive bully isn't likely to care. The person who must deliver the bad news is put in the untenable position of being forced to deliver bad news to people he or she know will react badly. He or she doesn't like the news any more than the recipient but it's his or her job and not doing it will bring the wrath of the Tyrant. Sadly, the bearer of bad news, in the Tyrant culture, is typically one of the first to die.

The frat house culture

The frat house culture is characterized by man-children behaving badly. The denigration of women is seldom subtle and even Human Resources takes a "laissez fare attitude of "boys will be boys".

In this environment professionalism is practically nonexistent and just like a poorly disciplined fraternity hazing, bullying, and establishing a pecking order are common if not pervasive.

In this culture bad actors are often protected by executives and the result can create a powder keg environment. When a woman is having marital problems one or more of the "frat brothers" will swoop in with a sympathetic shoulder on which to cry.

The situation can be made even worse when an emotionally troubled woman chooses to get romantically involved with someone in a position of power in an effort to advance her career (personally I never had such an issue since the number of women willing to sleep their way to the bottom part of the middle is scarce.) The estranged lover or husband feels that he can't compete with a man outside his societal station and reasons that while he may not have money, fancy clothes, or a country club membership he does have a Glock, a fifth of Old Granddad, and the guts to show those people.

The Pressure Cooker

When most of us think of the Pressure Cooker work environment we think of the high-stakes and fast pace of Wall Street or something similar, but in many cultures, there is a pervasive feeling that your only as good as your last sale or project and that your job hangs by a thread. The bosses in these environments cultivate a chronic sense of unease and high stress---the harder they push people the more money they themselves make. As indicated in another area of this book, I worked at a place where one top executive openly bragged about firing the lowest 10% of performers.

This human leaking colonoscopy bag of excrement thought that this made him a tough leader, when in fact it just sapped the motivation of the workforce and drove fear to every area of the company. For the pressure cooker to take hold the managers must simultaneously convince the workers that they will never have it this good anywhere else. Eventually, a worker snaps and explodes. Most don't go on a killing spree but companies that perpetuate this pressure-cooker environment are basically daring a worker to go on a killing spree.

The shadow of the leader

Not all bullies are at the top of the organization, in fact, anyone at any level can be a bully. Bullying in the workplace, particularly by a supervisor, can be subtle or overt, but if it is tolerated than the bully is emboldened to escalate his or her behavior. People take their cues from the leaders of the organization (nobody ever wrote a bestseller called "Dress for Complete and Utter Failure".)

The key to achieving success in an organization is to curry favor by imitating the leader of the organization—this phenomenon is often referred to as "the Shadow of the Leader" and it can be powerful and pervasive in a corporate culture. As someone once said to me, "what the admiral finds interesting the rest of us find fascinating." There's good news in this because while a bullying boss can create a climate of fear, a kind and nurturing boss can not only tear down a culture of tyranny but can build a culture that demands respect for subordinates and peers.

I once worked for a CEO who was a kind, spiritual and genuinely good person who was tasked with turning a company around. The task didn't suit him because it meant that he would end up laying off half the workforce, eliminating a ridiculously generous bonus criteria and replacing it with one based on whether or not the company made money. He saved the company, but many people despised him. He went on to join or found (I'm not too sure which) a corporate chaplaincy consultancy that teaches top executives how to be good business people and still be good and decent people; it's a job that suits him well and unlike many of the bosses I've mentioned in this book, I wish him every success. Sadly, he was replaced by a boorish buffoon with the manners and demeanor of a closed-head injured warthog.

What's the Difference Between A Single Shooter Event and "Going Postal"?

In his book, *Beyond Going Postal: Shifting from Workplace Tragedies and Toxic Work Environment to Safe and Healthy Organization,* Dr. Steve Musacco says, "Many people have asked: Why is there so much stress and workplace tragedies in the U.S. Postal Service? The answer to these questions is because the postal culture embraces and reflects core values that center on achieving bottom-line results with little or no regard for employee participation, respect, dignity, or fairness. Additionally, there is little or no accountability for the actions of top management in the Postal Service.

Many postal facilities consequently have toxic work environments, and they can be a catalyst or trigger for serious acts of workplace violence, including homicide and suicide. The associated rewards system for behavior consistent with the postal culture core values, moreover, enables systemic organizational and individual bullying of employees at all levels of the organization.[15] Dr. Musacco was not alone in his beliefs, and other studies painted the post office as a quasi-military operation that used many of the same tactics that the military does that sent many workers to the breaking point.

The point is, that going postal was the result of a uniquely toxic work culture that the United States Post Office has taken steps to correct. In fact, the last postal attack was on December 23, 2017 where a postal worker beat the postmaster to death over his pending dismissal, was the first fatal workplace violence in the US Postal Service since 2006 [16]. This latest case puts the United States Postal Service on a par with most any other workplace.

The Office of the Postmaster General has taken steps to curtail the shootings by addressing root causes, and a lot can be learned from these measures (There were 21 incidents of Post Office Shootings from 1983 to 2006, with most clustered in the mid 1990's and 1980s) the USPS has taken. According to the Office of the Postmaster General's official website, "subsequent to the Postal Service's response, members of the

---

[15] *Source: Beyond Going Postal: Shifting from Workplace Tragedies and Toxic Work Environment to Safe and Healthy Organization, January 27, 2009*

[16] *Source: https://en.wikipedia.org/wiki/List_of_postal_killings*

House Committee on Oversight and Government Reform requested that we review the Postal Service's workplace violence program and validate the Postal Service's March 2015 response."

Our objectives were to evaluate whether the Postal Service adequately identified, reviewed, reported, and addressed employee assaults; and to validate the Postal Service's response to Congress. Our audit covers workplace violence incidents that occurred from September 1, 2013, through September 2, 2015, a period during which the Postal Inspection Service recorded 789 workplace violence cases nationwide.

What the OIG Found

The Postal Service has a comprehensive workplace violence program to identify, review, report, and address employee assaults nationwide. The Postal Service and Postal Inspection Service appropriately addressed all workplace violence cases in the six selected districts reviewed. In these districts, the Postal Inspection Service investigated 145 cases, 60 of which involved Postal Service employees as assailants. The Postal Service imposed administrative actions, including suspensions and notices of removal, in all 60 cases, as required.

However, opportunities exist to enhance the workplace violence program. Specifically, Postal Service officials did not always record all incidents of workplace violence in the tracking system, effectively use threat teams to review assault outcomes and develop preventive measures and display all workplace violence posters and publications used to educate employees on identifying and reporting workplace violence incidents in postal facilities.

These and other issues occurred in the six districts we reviewed because:

- District Human Resources managers responsible for maintaining the tracking system database did not

118

ensure responsible officials entered assault complaints into the tracking system as required. In addition, the policy does not give specific instructions regarding the deadline for doing so.

- There were no controls to ensure that threat assessment team activities were completed, including required training.

- Facility managers were not fully aware of the requirements to display workplace violence posters and were not required to check periodically that all workplace violence posters were displayed.

The Postal Service was responsive to Congress by providing information regarding how they prevent and respond to workplace violence incidents in reporting 68 employee sexual assaults that resulted in EEO complaints. However, all sexual assaults do not result in EEO complaints. As such, the Postal Service did not report 10 sexual assault cases investigated by the Postal Inspection Service for the period October 1, 2012, through December 1, 2014. Although the Postal Service qualified its response as pertaining only to EEO complaints, the inclusion of related Postal Inspection Service cases would have provided a more complete response.

Further, the Postal Service could not rely on the tracking system as a central repository for sexual assault data because officials were not always recording the data in the tracking system, as required. To gather complete data for its response to Congress, the Postal Service should have reviewed the tracking system, EEO complaints, and Postal Inspection Service cases.

As a result of these conditions, there is an increased risk the Postal Service will not effectively analyze data and identify trends to address workplace violence incidents. Furthermore, without a single accurate source of data in this critical area of employee safety, it is more difficult to determine where problems exist and develop preventive measures.[17]

Does the USPC have the problem of workplace violence figured out? Well the relatively few postal workers who have gone on killing rampages would to seem to indicate that if they haven't solved the problem, they are certainly making progress. This section may be little more than trivia, but I thought it worth including, because most people who use the term "going postal" don't have a clue what they're talking about, and we have enough stupidity as it stands.

Either way, I'm nice to postal workers just to be on the safe side.

---

[17] https://www.uspsoig.gov/document/postal-service-workplace-violence-program

Chapter 6: Creating a Culture Of Resiliency

Resilience is all the rage right now, and for good reasons. For one, it is backed by a wide body of research and excellent books that are easy to read and understand. A good portion of resilience is, without saying it overtly is focusing on reducing stress, as we will discuss, how we manage our stress individually, AND how we look to decrease unnecessary stress in our corporate cultures.

In a cultural sense, resilience is an individual or a culture's ability to rebound and bounce back after setbacks—whether it be a poor performance evaluation, or a tragedy in the work. Resilience is more than just the latest Human Resource buzzword—resilient people tend to stay healthy, have fewer workplace injuries, recover from sickness when they do get ill, lose their tempers less frequently, and live happier, more peaceful, and low stress lives.

Even the friendliest parents will tell their children not to talk to strangers. Why? Aren't strangers just friends we haven't met yet? Of course, we warn our children about strangers because of a potential threat, not an actual threat. Our brains treat the nonverbal, subconscious input in the exact same way, when in doubt, sound the alarm.

The brain figures that it's better to have chemicals that we don't need than it is to need chemicals that we don't have; but this is not necessarily a healthy outlook. What's worse is that because our brains respond to the absence of information in the same way it does to real danger indicators. Our brains must assume that information that is not in the danger database is a threat; if it assumes a perception is benign when it is malignant the body is completely vulnerable.

But if the brain assumes the perception is malignant when it is actually benign the body is still ready for action and assumes no real risk. A lack of information from an authority figure will lead to paranoia. If our bosses don't talk to us we convince ourselves that our boss doesn't like us. If the silence continues we may convince ourselves that our boss intends to fire us. Left unchecked, this fear may make us dislike our boss to the point where we quit or act out and get fired.

All of this, hardwired, instinctual behavior makes us less resilient and all of benefits of being resilient are replaced with opposite effects, and creating a resilient workplace becomes essential.

To complicate matters, non-verbal warnings may not even come from our own senses, often we are victims of "herd stress". Herd stress is where an individual picks up the stress of his or her surroundings. Watch a documentary on the animals of Africa and you will see an excellent example of herd stress. A herd of gazelles stands leisurely grazing. Suddenly one tenses at a hint of danger. Within seconds the whole herd is on full alert and in the blink of an eye the herd stampedes as one, out of harm's way.

Are we humans so different? When we pick up nonverbal cues that indicate that someone around us is stressed, we become stressed. Why? Because our brains sense that even though it can detect no danger, perhaps someone else in the tribe has perceived danger. Our bodies will react without waiting to see if the threat is real. Think of this as the "lookout reflex". Our bodies rely on "look outs" to warn it of dangers that it either has not detected or has not yet cataloged as dangers.

Picture our senses as our bodies' radar. We gather information about our physical environment and scan for dangers. If our senses pick up no sign of danger we are completely relaxed. If on the other hand, our bodies detect potential dangers it puts our bodies on alert; the level of alertness corresponds to the level of the perceived danger. The United States military uses a system to rate security threats on a five-point scale. Defcon 5 represents the lowest level of threat while Defcon 1 represents the highest. This is an apt analogy for our bodies system for evaluating danger. When we are relaxing and having fun our internal radar has sensed no threats and so it offers no reaction, it's at Defcon 5. But as the subconscious mind identifies potential threats, it moves us to a more heightened state, Defcon 4 if the threats need to be monitored but prove no immediate threat, Defcon 3 if the threats are more serious and so on.

Anything that interferes with our ability to correctly monitor the dangers around us causes de facto stress. Listening to music so loud that we can't hear an ambulance siren is very stressful, for example. Our internal radar is jammed so we must drop to Defcon 3 since that is the only way our subconscious can be sure that we are protected. Great! So we have to sit around in silence or stress will kill us, right? Silence can also stress us.   Nature teems with noises from crickets chirping to birds singing.   Silence in the forest usually signals a danger is looming.   The last thing one hears before the leopard attacks is an unnerving silence before the roar.

By surrounding yourself with silence you may be adding to your stress.   Our bodies need and expect to hear some ambient noise, without some noise our radar may believe the senses are malfunctioning, or that the lack of noise is just the silence before the roar.   Remember our brains didn't construct the danger database in a vacuum, rather it assigned meaning to each of the inputs it received.   The popularity of recordings of natural sounds (waves crashing, wolves howling, rain falling) is testament to the soothing effects of nature.

So much of the information we receive is non-verbal and subconscious that sometimes we see some "unexplained" phenomenon, like psychic flashes and premonitions.   Have you ever had a dream that foretold the future?   Predicted the death of a loved one?   While there are cases where such phenomenon cannot be readily dismissed in many cases these psychic emanations are nothing more mysterious than our subconscious mind reading clues that our conscious minds miss and predicting a likely outcome.

Take the psychic flash that foretells the death of someone you know.   Isn't it plausible that your internal radar picked up nonverbal cues from the person (subtle changes in skin color, behavior, tone of voice, weight, etc,) that gave your subconscious a clue that all was not well with the person's physical condition, even though the person may not have been aware of his or her own weakening physical state?

Why Worry: Stress that We Deliberately Create
Another common source of stress is what I call "predictive stress". Predictive stress arises from the common practice of

trying to relieve pressures of worrying by asking, "what's the worst thing that could happen?" Asking this question is incredibly stress producing as we now add a whole list of calamities to our worries.

It's not bad enough that we worried that our boss didn't like us, now well-meaning but dim-witted friends introduce the worst-case scenario and we add being fired, losing our homes and become destitute and diseased homeless nomads driven mad by life's luxuries lost. Gee that's a cheery thought, thank you for adding to my gloom. It makes sense that if we don't have a complete picture of a situation that we would have to prepare for the worst-case scenario.

The problem with this practice is that the worst-case scenario is seldom the mostly likely scenario. Instead of picturing the worst-case scenario, we should picture and plan for, the most likely scenario. When we plan for the most likely scenario, it's prudent to prepare some contingency plans (saving money for a rainy day, for example) but we need to stop our Armageddon thinking and concentrate on real issues and things we can do to minimize our risks.

Take for instance, the prospect of losing your job. Economic conditions, management decisions and a host of other factors that could contribute to losing our jobs are completely beyond our control, so worrying about these and obsessing about them is a complete waste of time: the stress consumes our energy and provides us with nothing of value in return. Resiliency efforts seek to provide tools to teach people to see opportunities and silver linings. For example, a highly resilient person doesn't waste energy worrying about losing his or her job, Instead of worrying about the prospect of losing a job, we need to make contingency plans.

In all the environments we discussed before there is a common denominator: high stress and an acceptance of abhorrent behavior. A resilient culture is marked by:

- **Compassion.** Organizations that are highly resilient encourage compassionate management. These organizations don't have a binary "right/wrong" view of behavior, and communicate openly and honestly with workers to determine the causes of undesirable behaviors before deciding on a course of action. Human error—irrespective of the outcome—is consoled. Take for example, the case where a nurse accidentally gave adult doses of a medicine to newborns. Several infants died. A complete investigation found that the adult and infant medications were stored side by side in identical packaging (except for small print indicating whether it was for adults or infants.) Virtually anyone could have made this same mistake, and the system had so many poor designs that failure was all but certain. If it wasn't this nurse who made the mistake someone else would eventually had done the same thing. What is the compassionate response? Console the nurse and reassure her (in this case) that the deaths, while a result of her error, were all but unavoidable. The hospital took immediate action to work with the manufacturer to design noticeably different packaging and to segregate adult medications (of all kinds) from pediatric medication).

    Compassion extends far beyond forgiving human error and includes policies that go beyond regulatory requirements for family leave or similar situations. A resilient culture provides resources for things like elder or childcare, unlimited sick and bereavement leave[18]. I have worked in several companies that had formal bereavement policies that were enforced compassionately. When my mother died, the owner of the company not only sent flowers and came to the funeral, but he also told me not to worry about what the policy said, but for me to take a much time as I needed. Similarly, while working at another job, my father died and again, not only did the owner of the company attend the services at the funeral home AND the funeral, but so did all of the company's executives, AND my teammates. It was very touching to me because the trip for many of them was 50 miles one way or more, and I had only been on the job for less than 8 months.

Still, another employer insisted that I take more time off when my brother-in-law died and even though I didn't feel I needed it, it helped me grieve. In all these cases, the compassion demonstrated by my managers, executives, and colleagues made me feel more comfortable, loyal, and more aligned with the company's values.

If you want to create a culture of resilience, review your policies and ask yourself if they were borne of compassion or designed to protect the company from liars, cheats, and malingerers, because if you treat your

---

[18] That statement has some of you freaking out. Who will come to work if we provide unlimited paid sick or bereavement leave?!?!?! I once worked at a company that had a very simple sick leave policy: If you're sick, stay home. (A manager was always within his or her right to ask for a doctor's excuse, but encouraged to do so only if he or she was worried about the worker's health.) The average sick leave taken in a company of 6,000 was .5 hours per employee per year. When managers complained that there was no sick leave policy Human Resources acquiesced and each employee was allotted 5 sick days a year. Within six months the sick leave rate had risen to an average of 4.5 days a year. Was anything accomplished in doing this? Or was the company better off with its previous more compassionate approach.

workers as liars, cheats, and malingerers you will end up with a company filled with liars, cheats, and malingerers. There is a great book, *Raving Fans: A Revolutionary Approach to Customer Service* By Ken Blanchard and Sheldon Bowles. The book demonstrates many of the characteristics of a resilient culture but that is not its intent. I cite it just for all you uptight managers who mistake compassion for weakness. In the book, a character goes into a department store and is shocked to learn that he can take as much merchandise into the changing room as he wants. He questions the manager, asking incredulously, if the story was unconcerned about theft. The manager laughs and said that they have found that only a small percent of their customers are likely to steal, and it seemed downright insulting to treat 99% of the customers as potential thieves when only 1% stole. Expect greatness from your workers and they will seldom disappoint you. Very few will cheat the system so manage those few who do.

In his book, *Resilient: How To Grow An Unshakable Calm, Strength, And Happiness,* Rick Hanson, Ph.D defines compassion as "warm-hearted concern for suffering and the desire to relieve it if you can" and further adds *"Compassion is a psychological resource—an inner strength— that can be developed over time."* As you review your policies ask yourself what your company is doing to build your workforce's psychological resources.

- **Mindfulness.** Hanson identifies mindfulness as the second element of Resilience. In short, mindfulness is the practice of focusing your mind on positives, and training yourself to overcome the natural tendency to be pessimistic. In my unpublished book, *Why Do We Tell Our Children Not To Take Candy From Strangers*

When Everyone Knows That Strangers Have the Best Candy? I explore the very real dynamic of why we are predisposed to pessimism and distrust. I have started many presentations asking the simple question: why don't we let our children take candy from strangers?

The answer is simple pragmatism and risk to reward ratio. Four possible conditions exist:

1. A stranger wants to harm our child and succeeds

2. A stranger wants to harm our child and does not succeeds.

3. A stranger does not want to harm our child and gives them a harmless treat.

4. A stranger does not want to harm our child and our child does not engage with the stranger.

In all of these scenarios a stranger could easily harm our child, by telling our children to avoid strangers we are able to avoid a horrendous outcome. So, despite the fact that most strangers are not trying to harm our children we chose to allow our suspicions to guide our behavior. This pessimism is more than just a defense mechanism against disappointment—it actually creates physiological pathways that make us less resilient. Think of the stress of always being alert to dangers; people tend to see the Fight/Flight/Freeze response as a binary response (we either rapidly react to danger in one of these ways or we don't) but we know intuitively that most strangers don't want to hurt our children.

- **Continuous Learning.** Learning helps us overcome our natural tendency to expect, and prepare for, disaster. Amazingly, learning doesn't just provide us new knowledge or skills, but it also improves our neural pathways and allows us to build the skills we need to see the silver lining in situations instead of the potential dangers. Optimism is a skill that needs to be learned, but before you can learn to be optimistic you have to unlearn the default setting of pessimism that our subconscious has programed for us. Abraham Lincoln reputedly said (and this is in dispute by pedantic mouth-breathers with nothing better to do) "We're just about as happy as we make up our minds to be," As it turns out, it appears that not only was Abe right on this account but his quote is backed up by hard science.

- **Resources to Build Physical Strength.** Fitness centers were popular in the late 1980s and early 1990s but companies, citing the cost of maintaining facilities and the lack of use by workers, phased these programs out. But programs designed to improve workers' physical fitness are making a rebound. Scientists are finding that working out not only improves your immune system and helps prevent or stave off adverse medical conditions but will actually make you happier, and therefore more resilient.

- **Stress Management.** Stress management will always be a hot topic. Stress, simply put, is our body's way of protecting us from danger. Without stress we would blissfully roast our hands against a hot stove, or lop our way into oncoming traffic where smiling motorists would mow us down. We owe our lives to stress. When stress is properly applied to our bodies it saves our lives. We yank our hands away from hot stoves, leap in panicked jerks out of the path of oncoming traffic as the freaked-out motorist careens wildly

130

through traffic to avoid us. Yes, stress is an important part of our survival. But what about when stress is misused, misinterpreted, or misdirected by our bodies (did I miss any "misses"?) The same reflexes designed to preserve our fleshy behinds turns on our bodies like a jilted ex-lover.

Most of the information our brains receive comes to us through our subconscious. In order for us to be able to focus and concentrate on abstract tasks our brains automate many of our routine tasks. Picture your brain as a computer filled with thousands of software programs that automate the simpler tasks, and even some tasks that are not so simple. How many of us have to stop and think about the physical steps required to turn a doorknob, start a car, or drive to work. We do all these things without thinking because our brain has automated these tasks.

The old joke about not being able to walk and chew gum at the same time is funny precisely because our brains have so automated these tasks that to not be able to do both at the time is ludicrous. While the conscious mind doesn't bother with the mundane, the subconscious works overtime to get us through our day. In addition to running these "subroutines" our brains must sort through tons of information that it receives and route some of it to our conscious minds while filing most of it away in our subconscious where it is compared by the nervous system against our "database of danger."

Forgive my melodrama, but I think the analogy is an apt one. As infants we come into this world with very little information; we're helpless. Through a concerted effort on the part of our brains we gather as much information as we can as quickly as we can. We quickly learn that a hot stove is far too dangerous to be trifled with and so we file away in our subconscious any inputs—visual, aural, oral, tactile, and olfactory— that are even remotely related to the danger we call a hot stove. Our subconscious even writes a program that cause us to remove our hand from a hot stove so fast that we have removed ourselves from the danger before our conscious minds even realizes what's happening. Our subconscious has saved us using what scientists call the fight-flight reflex. [19]

The fight-flight response is our bodies' way of protecting us from the all the dangers that we have filed away in the "danger database". As we our bombarded with information our brains sift through the small percentage that is necessary for our cognitive functions, or in other words the things that require us to think about, for instance, reading. Do you find it difficult to concentrate in a room filled with noise? Is it more difficult for you to read in when surrounded by a flurry of activity? If so, the difficulty likely arises from your brain trying to sort through this input to determine whether or not a danger is present.

In the time you are taking to read this, your brain is being deluged with sensory input. Perhaps a fluorescent light is buzzing nearby or maybe a television plays off in the distance. While you aren't conscious of the input, your subconscious is carefully and quickly reviewing the information and checking it against your danger database.

---

[19] *The term has evolved to Fight-Flight-Freeze but I see Flight and Freeze as essentially the same response, we either adopt an aggressive stance or a passive/defensive stance.*

In most cases these inputs are harmless and your subconscious doesn't bother you with them. In some cases, these inputs match a danger in the database and trigger a conscious response. In still other cases, the input doesn't provide enough information for a definitive conclusion to be made and the brain has to assume a "better safe than sorry" posture. In these cases, the brain prepares the body for the worst-case scenario and the result is stress.

Just as touching a hand to a hot stove elicits a rapid response where we jerk our hand from harm's way, so too does our body react to subtler threats although in far less dramatic ways.

Whenever our bodies perceive danger our brains activate the "flight or fight" reflex. First it our bodies give us an energy rush as it releases stored sugar and fats into the bloodstream. Next our brains increase our breathing to supply more oxygen to the blood—oxygen that will be needed to give our bodies the short-term boost it will need to combat the danger. Our heart rate then accelerates to provide more blood to the muscles. Newly flush with more blood, our muscles tense for action.

More blood is quickly supplied to these muscles as the body reroutes the blood from the hands and feet. Blood is also routed to the brain and away from the stomach and digestion stops. Our senses become more acute and actively scan for more signs of danger. Finally, alertness heightens to the point where it becomes difficult to focus. Our bodies turn into finely honed killing machines ready to strike down danger in its tracks. Unfortunately, not all triggers are, in fact, dangers.

Most of us have heard of mothers who experience brief moments of superhuman strength and lift a car off a trapped child, a testament (whether factual or not) to the benefits of the fight-flight reflex. But what about instances where the threat isn't real? What effect does the fight-flight reflex in imagined, or misperceived threats have on our bodies? The body reacts to a threat that isn't there the same way it does to real threats, it gets our bodies ready to bust a head or bust a move. In the cases where the treat is imaginary, or chronic, our brains flood our bodies with toxic chemicals that we don't really need and can't use and so our bodies are left to deal with these chemicals the same way it deals with other poisons.

Remember the story of the Sword of Damocles? In this legend, Damocles expresses his envy for the life of a king he was visiting, marveling at the luxurious palace, array of servants, and beautiful women at the king's disposal. To prove a point (to put it mildly) the king orders his servants to suspend a sword above Damocles' head with a single string (more than kind of a dick move if you ask me). The king then tells Damocles that this is what the king's life is like; always wondering if the string will break and he will be killed.

For many of us, our lives are like the Sword of Damocles, and our bodies react to the stress of wondering when the dangers we continuously perceive will make their moves and force us into action.

Stress is designed to protect us, so why does it cause us harm? The fight-flight reflex was designed as a short-term solution to an acute, life-threatening situation, by kicking our bodies into overdrive, but the bulb that burns twice as bright burns half as long. Instead of

134

release a massive does of chemicals, we instead release low-level doses that wear our bodies out.

When our fight flight reflex is activated our brains become miniature chemical plants as an area of the brain stem releases of a variety of chemicals. Norepinephrine, a hormone, that in turn causes the Adrenal glands to release and pump out Adrenaline. Adrenaline increases our heart rate and raises our metabolism in anticipation hearts beat faster, our blood pressure increase, our pulses to race, us to sweat, and for us to breath heavily.

The brain also reroutes our blood from the stomach to our muscles and other vital areas of the body while it releases blood sugar, lactic acid and other chemicals, all to get the body ready to pound a mugger's head in, or to run like a rabbit. These toxic chemicals are effectively toxins that give our bodies a quick jump-start. This "shot of adrenaline" is critical to our survival but this barrage of chemicals affects our emotions and leaves us feeling anxious, worried, and even paranoid—even when the danger isn't real.

We tend to think of the Fight-Flight Reflex as an all or nothing proposition, but is it? What about small dangers that we encounter that don't escalate into a full-blown crisis? In these cases the brain still releases chemicals and prepares our bodies for battle. Blood is rerouted, smaller amount of chemicals are released instead of an immediate response the brain gradually puts us on alert, effectively changing our body chemistry and putting a long-term stress on our major biological systems.

Let's again take a look at what is happening to our bodies: our heart rate increases. An accelerated heart rate is useful in a crisis but a chronic increase leads to high blood pressure. We breathe faster providing more oxygen, but when the condition is chronic it causes chest pains from a tired, strained diaphragm. Digestion stops as blood leaves the stomach; this causes a variety of digestive problems and aggravates ulcers. Blood leaves the hands, head, and feet, which causes headache, and cold hands and feet. Coagulation of the blood increases, which increases the likelihood of blood clots and strokes. Muscles tense in anticipation of an attack; which leads to chronic muscle pain and fatigue.

In short, if we expose ourselves to low-grade stresses we use our body in a way in which it was never intended and it wears our. Just as a building that was designed to withstand a great force all at once will gradually fall apart from years of light wear, so to will our bodies fall apart from constant exposure to stress.

Some of you maybe thinking, "okay this makes sense, but I don't exactly have a whole lot of danger in my life, but I still have a whole lot of stress." I doubt any of us have no dangers around us, although I grant you most of the dangers that our bodies perceive aren't real.

Again, most communication is nonverbal, in other words, most information we gather about our surroundings comes from our senses, and not from what we read or that is spoken to us. Our senses are barraged with input that our brain sorts and filters and decides what is important. We need only take a moment, close our eyes and listen to the noises in the room. How many previously unnoticed noises do you hear? All our senses are gathering data at a blinding speed and storing it in the wonderful and amazing database of our brain. Some of these inputs the brain decides are worthy of the attention of the conscious mind while others it stores in our subconscious mind for later retrieval and use if necessary.

The brain rightfully judges much of the input from our senses as benign, while other information is matched up against our database to see if it is indicative of danger. If one smells smoke, one is likely to investigate the cause. Why? Is the smell of smoke so unpleasant that we should immediately eradicate it? No. Why then do we investigate the smell of smoke? To be sure there is no danger of fire. So what does any of this have to do with stress? As infants we gather and catalog sensory input, some of these inputs we categorize as harmless and others we categorize as harmful. We are confronted with many things we've programmed ourselves to see as potential hazards. Take for instance the baby crying on an airplane. We know that babies cry for a variety of reasons that have nothing to do with any sort of danger to us, yet the baby's cry produces physiological responses in our body because our subconscious catalog equates crying with danger.

But in many cases, our poor brains don't have enough information to make an informed decision as to whether or not sound the alarms so it assumes the worst. In the early days of humanity mankind didn't have the luxury of mistakes, if Grog ate the blue food and died, the rest of the tribe steered clear of blue food, reasoning it was better to miss out on a culinary delight that it is to die an agonizing death from ingesting poison. The idea that what you don't know can kill you is hard wired into our brains, and the human animal has adapted to this such that if we don't have enough information we fill in the gaps with the worst case scenario.

Superstitions grew out of man's need to accurately predict the outcome of serious situations, like a major battle or the harvest crops. Desperate to predict the future, man turned to oracles, mystics, and fortune tellers. Primitive societies didn't have a whole lot of stress as we know it, but they had their fair share of death.

The optimists among us are now shaking their heads and decrying this as heresy, but consider this situation: your boss tells everyone in the department (except you) that they are to be in a mandatory meeting at 9:00 a.m. the next morning. When you ask your boss if you need to be there, your boss says, "No, I just need to see everyone else." You ask similarly tight-lipped co-workers who tell you "they aren't allowed to talk about the meeting, or what it's about."

Now, do you ask yourself, is the purpose of the meeting to plan a surprise party for you or is some sinister plot afoot? Is this example really so absurd? What responsible parent tells a child "if a stranger offers you a ride, you take it! You never know when another stranger will be by and the next stranger may not offer!"

- **Fun.** Resilient cultures are fun places to work. Work and fun are not mutually exclusive. People who have fun at work, celebrate successes, and have a sense of humor are more resilient than those who are not (so people who have complained about my use of humor during my speeches and presentations and in my writing can suck it—I'm not unprofessional I'm resilient.)

Social Support. Resilient cultures openly encourage the celebrations of life's great moments and love and support in times of tragedy. These activities are voluntary and organic, not mandatory. A friend of mine used to work for a company that tried to force teamwork and a social support network by having mandatory and unpaid weekend canoe trip. She hated canoeing and didn't much care for her coworkers. She didn't go and was gigged on her performance review for missing it. This is so incredibly stupid I don't even have a comment or a joke. The story itself is more sad and Kafkaesque than I could ever make it. It is so ludicrous that even I the king of tall tales lacks the imagination to make it up

Resilient Cultures and positive work environments help prevent workplace single shooter events:

1. Mentally Unstable Individuals are given the care and support that they need, and

2. Potential targets are supported by a network of caring coworkers who can both steer them towards the resources that they need and can watch out for the security of the potential target, and more importantly the resilient environment provides both the unstable loner and the potential target a legitimately caring environment and reduces the risk of workplace violence.

Chapter 7: Policies and Procedures to Prevent and Protect

It's been a while since I threw in a disclaimer about how I am not a lawyer and that you should run ANY policy past your legal counsel before putting it into practice. There I said it. If you don't check with the people on your payroll who are there specifically to keep you out of hot water, then don't come whining to me when some idea that I threw out there gets you sued. Now, that having been said (again)...

Even though you may have taken great pains to screen likely perpetrators or targets of workplace violence there is still a chance that one or two might slip through your stopgaps. What's more likely, however, is that someone you hired—through circumstances, life experience, or some other reason—changes. Divorce, the loss of a loved one, a serious illness, stress, alcoholism, or simply poor choices can change an otherwise stable individual into a candidate who, when confronted by the right triggers, can become a single shooter or a target. Unfortunately, or fortunately, (depending on your outlook) you cannot terminate a worker's employment because of something he or she MIGHT do. But since you know the warning signs of a workplace single shooter event, your policies can not only set a tone for expected behaviors but can also prevent the development of environmental conditions that make workplace violence more likely.

Employee Assistance Programs

One of the strongest preventive measures you can take is to implement an Employee Assistance Program (EAP). An EAP allows workers to talk to trained professionals about problems at work or at home. The information is confidential [20] and the EAP providers have access to solutions for a variety of problems an employee may have from referrals to daycare or elder care providers to mental health providers. In many cases an EAP can help employees deal with the "little issues" which, if ignored, can otherwise grow into major problems.

---

[20] *Within reason. An EAP operator has a moral and often legal responsibility to notify the company and law enforcement in some circumstances, for example if someone confesses his or her intention to commit a single shooter event.*

I remember a case during the great recession where a major global employer did a study of the nature of the calls to their EAP line only to find that the vast majority of calls had shifted from workers complaining about issues with coworkers or supervisors to employees worried about money and losing their jobs. Whatever the emotional crisis a good EAP will have resources (like counselling for example) to decrease the risk of someone becoming a workplace shooter. The EAP can provide resources that can teach employees coping skills and provide tools for workers to deal with their issues without resorting to violence.

Employee Resilience Training

Resilience is the ability for people to bounce back from tragedy or hardship. Many companies are investing in training and coaching in resilience to help their workers to cope with personal tragedies or work hardships.

In her September 18th article in *Psychology Today, How to Build Your Resilience*[20], Dr. Ellen Henderson says: "Importantly, resilience is an acquired skill, not a you're-born-with-it-or-you're-not trait, which means whether you sink or swim is actually dependent on a skill that can be taught and learned with time. So how do you make sure you come out on top? Here are six ways to make like a rubber band and bounce back.

Tip #1: Let yourself feel lousy every once in a while.

You heard that right. We've all heard the cliché

---

[20] Source:https://www.psychologytoday.com/us/blog/how-be-yourself/201709/how-build-your-resilience

encouragement: "When life gives you lemons, make lemonade!" But rah-rah motivational slogans often feel useless, like sunglasses on a cloudy day.

True resilience doesn't mean you never get discouraged. If you never encounter painful struggle, you never get to discover your resilience. This is why pain is almost universal among the resilient—it happens.

Therefore, resilience isn't about masking your pain and pretending everything is peachy—you're human, not a machine. In short, what matters isn't how you feel in the moment, it's that you overcome it and stand back up. That's resilience.

Tip #2: Know that you're the only one who can control your fate.

In 1955, the psychologist Dr. Emmy Werner began a study that would last more than 40 years. She and her colleagues began to follow every child—almost 700 of them—born that year on the Hawai'ian island of Kauai.

Kauai in the 1950s was not a privileged place. Many of the kids were raised in poverty, had unstable, chaotic families, and had mothers who never got a high school diploma. But despite all this, by the age of 40, one-third of the group was, as the study said, "competent, confident, and caring." They defied the odds—they all were employed, had stable lives, and never came into trouble with the law. Their accomplishments equaled or surpassed many of the kids who grew up in more privileged environments. The researchers itched to know: how did they beat the odds? What was the key ingredient to their resilience?

Again, it's complicated. Some of it was luck, some of it was having at least one emotionally stable and loving family member to look out for them, and some of it was finding an emotional home in a civic organization, at school, or at church.

But the most important thing the resilient kids had was something called an internal locus of control, meaning that these kids believed that they, not their circumstances, were in the driver's seat. They believed they were the controllers of their own future, and the circumstances they were put in were not a deterring factor. The researchers noted an example of this was that resilient kids with a dysfunctional family were good at "recruiting" surrogate parents, whether a youth minister, a trusted teacher, or even a friend's parent.How can you apply this to your life? In short, take decisive action. It's tempting to use fate as an excuse for your future, but take control as best you can.

Tip #3: Keep yourself value-centered.

It's all fine and good to make executive decisions, but if the right decision isn't clear, it can be easy to make mistakes. A handful of studies have found that having a moral compass—an internal system of values and ethics—goes along with higher resilience. Strong ethics and morality seems to give purpose to our lives, which in turn gives rise to resilience. So maybe in the bigger picture that Boston cream doughnut was nothing to get worked up about?

Tip #4: Recharge with a workout.

Dealing with setbacks can be exhausting, so it's important not just to push your way back too hard, but to rest and recharge along the way. You have full permission to recharge in any way you wish (marathoning Friends on the couch with a pint of Ben & Jerry's, just as an example), but maybe consider, between episodes, some exercise.

Exercise is often a mini metaphor for life's larger challenges: We set short-term goals that build mental momentum to reach larger goals in the long term. Pushing through on both good and bad days is resilience in action.

Plus, exercise heightens your mood and motivation levels, which directly relieves stress and puts us in a more positive mindset. It's the ultimate recharge, with the added bonus of feeling a little better about the aforementioned Ben & Jerry's.

Tip #5: Don't set unrealistic goals.

You may want to get rich, get famous, and spend little effort doing so, but part of resilience involves not setting ourselves up for failure. Indeed, in the Kauai study, one of the characteristics of the resilient adults was that they set realistic educational and career goals for themselves. If we set too many lofty goals, when we fall short of them, we will blame that failure on ourselves. So, keep the scale of your goals reasonable. Challenge yourself and aim high, of course, but be fair to yourself.

Tip #6: Express your feelings.

I know—it's cliché, but it works. According to a study of student nurses doing emotionally exhausting work in a literal life-or-death environment, those who were able to 1) draw on support from friends and colleagues, and 2) genuinely express their emotions from sorrow to frustration to joy, were less prone to burnout. They were able to continue the tough emotional work their job required. So, tell people you trust how you really feel. Be honest and authentic rather than trying to please everyone and you'll come out feeling relieved and sane.

It's only when obstacles arise that your resilience skills are called on. Even Barry Manilow made it through the rain. And so can you, with a secret weapon called resilience. [22]

----

[22] *A version of this piece originally appeared on Quick and Dirty Tips titled 6 Ways to Build Your Resistance.*

Access Policies

Every company should have a policy that delineates exactly who is authorized to be on the premises. These policies should be very specific as to who is allowed to be on the premises escorted, who is allowed on the premises unescorted, and who is not allowed on the premises.

Unescorted Personnel

Unescorted personnel are those employees who work for the company at that specific location. These people are employees who, through the course of their duties, must enter a specific suite of offices, warehouse or loading dock, or work zone. If the worker leaves the areas to which he or she has authorized access the employee must be escorted. Many organizations make the mistake of allowing employees from another company location (or another department) on the premises unescorted. Having keycards coded to the locations to which a worker is allowed to entered is very useful in this regard. This not only restricts a person's movement, but also can protect people from entering locations where hazardous work is performed.

Sometimes the strict definition of "unescorted personnel" is not as cut and dry as it may seem. Temporary or contract employees may be given an Identification Badge because they have a long-term contract with the company or return on a regular basis for meetings or to perform a specific service. In some cases, delivery people will also be granted unescorted access, but in these cases the unescorted access should only apply when the delivery person remains in his or her vehicle. If the driver is required to exit his or her vehicle, the driver should be met at the delivery point and escorted as long as he or she is outside the delivery vehicle.

Escorted Personnel

Escorted personnel are any individuals who are visiting the premises and who are not allowed to wander the halls without an employee who is authorized to be responsible for the actions and safety of the escorted person. The person who is escorted should be recorded in the visitor log and issued a temporary visitor's badge that must be returned before they depart. Escorted personnel include:

- Vendors
- Visitors (Including and especially ex-employees.)
- Law enforcement without a warrant [23]
- Emergency first responders [24]
- Job applicants with an appointment or interview

Unauthorized Personnel

Often times gatekeepers will encounter curiosity seekers, solicitors, or just plain weirdos who show up trying to gain access to the premises. Years ago, I worked in security, and while most of what I know about even the broadest points of their policies and procedures is literally top secret, I can tell you that when I was working the main gate, I saw my fair share of weirdos. From people just coming down, "just to check things out" to belligerent drunks insisting that they had every right to be there and challenging me to try and stop them, too pushy salespeople thinking they can con you into letting them in, to homeless indigents looking to take a short cut to innocent people who got lost and simply wanted directions. Whatever the case in your organization unauthorized means they don't get past the front gate, and in those cases where they do manage to sneak buy, ALL employees have a right and responsibility

---

[23] *Check with your legal counsel before making a determination as to the circumstances law enforcement agents can enter the premises without a warrant before entering the building.*

[24] *This is more to ensure that the first responders can get to the part of the building that they need too rather than a security precaution.*

to notify security and monitor the situation from a safe and secure distance.

Visitor Access

In addition to letting your workforce know who is and who is not an employee you need to clearly define who is an authorized visitor and who is not an authorized visitor. While it may seem harsh, one of the best policies you can have is a policy denying access to family members.

Sound cold-hearted? Remember the statistic from chapter one where the number one perpetrators of workplace violence against women in the workplace is a family member? A boyfriend or husband picking up his girlfriend/wife can wait at the front gate and be met there by his lunch date. There should be zero tolerance for piggy-backing through a code-locked door (the practice of more than one person entering through a door on one key card swipe.)

Solicitation Policies

It seems like every organization has a fundraiser going at any given time, and what's the harm in having mom or dad drag the goods into work to sell for their kids? Potentially plenty. No solicitation policies are often enacted to discourage Labor Union drives, but courts have ruled that "no solicitation" means exactly and precisely that—no selling cookies, or candles, or cosmetics, or distributing religious literature, or promoting hate groups, or...well you get the picture. NO means NO so the rule against solicitation must be applied to every instance of solicitation. Let your lazy kids sell their own overpriced candy, but don't allow their parents to come into work and pressure coworkers into buying it.

A no-soliciting policy will not be popular, but I sold it to organizations by saying, "the same policy that keeps people from trying to recruit you into a hate group or terrorist organization is the same policy that protects you from being pressured into a multi-level marketing scheme and unfortunately, it also means that you don't get to sell your kids' fundraising goods." People still hate the policy, but it does— when evenly and effectively enforced—protect companies from open hate speech and literature and helps you to create a work environment where people know that inciting hatred and violence will not be tolerated.

Dating Policies

Most of my women coworkers that I have asked out over the years seemed to have a no-dating-coworkers policy that only seemed to apply to me. But as we discussed earlier this is a murky, muddled, and confusing area of labor law that can differ from State to State. Even so, if you focus on the behaviors of the individuals while they are at work you are generally on solid legal footing. Of course, that's all well and good, except when one of these consulting adults is cheating on a spouse or domestic partner. This can put you into quite a quandary—if you do or say nothing you increase your risk of a workplace murder exponentially, but if you intercede you may violate the couple's right to privacy. So what can you do?

- **Communicate the Dangers of Workplace Relationships.** I should mention that I met my ex-wife at work. We were friends, but since I was a supervisor, I didn't think it wise to date her. When she (completely without my doing) became a supervisor, we started dating before I knew it, I was bamboozled into marrying her and for the next 20 years, she did her best to make my life a living hell. So, my advice has always been to avoid dating a co-worker because eventually, you could face the prospect of working with an angry ex-lover. Dear Abby once said, "dating in the workplace is like changing clothes in Macy's Department Store window—no matter how carefully you do it a whole lot of people are going to know about it." Your employee handbook, informed by and blessed by your legal council, should have a very clear policy on dating coworkers, and should, in dispassionate terms lay out the dangers and difficulties in having a workplace romance.

- **Instruct Supervisors to Monitor the Situation Closely.** Here again, you need to walk the tightrope between the aforementioned dilemma between protecting the workforce and avoiding invasion of privacy or even violating the law. As long as both of the involved workers are doing their jobs at a satisfactory level you should not get involved (unless you have a legal policy that forbids dating). Remind your supervisors that they cannot hold the couple to a higher standard of performance than other workers who are not dating co-workers.

Conflict Resolution Procedures

Having a standard and consistent conflict resolution process will go a long way toward nipping workplace violence in the bud. The good news here is that there are several fantastic methods already commercially available: one of these is the *Crucial Conversation Tools to Use When the Stakes Are High* series by Kerry Patterson Joseph Grenny, Ron McMillan, and Al Switzler. I won't get into the particulars of the books themselves (do yourself a favor and buy them) but what their methodology does is to remove most of the ugly emotions from disagreements. An organization to which I belonged had certified trainers in the methodology and all supervisors were required to complete the class, but more importantly, to demand that their teams followed the methodology. I remember I had a conflict with a woman I will call Stella. Before I was hired Stella had made a case to the department director as to why she should be my supervisor, but the director disagreed and told her in no uncertain terms that fact she was not. Stella was a domineering bull-in-a-china shop who insisted on giving me assignments and directions that I ignored. When I learned that Stella was complaining to coworkers about my job performance (which was none of her business) I went to my supervisor to complain. Before I could say more than a couple of words, my supervisor stopped me abruptly and asked me what Stella has said when I talked to her about my issues. I admitted that I had not spoken to her about the issue and my boss reviewed the conflict resolution process with me. She told me that she wanted me to make an appointment with Stella to have a "crucial conversation" and she wanted me to report back in a week to brief her on how the conversation went. Talking it through with Stella was the last thing I wanted to do, but I wanted to go back to my boss and tell her that I had disobeyed her instructions even less, so I reluctantly set a meeting with Stella.

When we met, she denied it at first, and I assertively asked her how then could she account for the fact that other coworkers had told me what she had been saying? I also told her flat out that if we couldn't settle this in this meeting, we both would have to meet with our mutual boss. Then she began to deflect and told me that I had to understand that she had been embroiled in a power struggle with my predecessor who treated her very badly.

I told her that we could talk about that when we finished our conversation, but at the moment we were talking about another matter—her talking about me behind my back and potentially harming my professional reputation. She began to cry. Unmoved, I told her that I thought she was deliberately trying to undermine me so that she could act as my supervisor that I felt betrayed by her behavior since I did nothing to invite it, and I wanted it to stop immediately. She apologized for her behavior and agreed that I didn't deserve it.

She promised that it would not happen again. It was very difficult for me to control my temper during this meeting, but I did, and by working a structured process I was able to channel my emotions into following the process. Not only did my relationship with Stella improve eventually we became good friends and collaborated often on projects without issues.

This organization's dedication to workers supporting each other and to never ignoring small and often petty differences was so pervasive that it was often difficult for new employees to adjust to the culture and first year turnover was above average.

Violence Policies

You should adopt a zero-tolerance policy for violence (that means dismissal even if the victim prefers to drop the matter) and that policy should include:

- **Physical acts of violence.** These acts should be clearly articulated to include any aggressive physical contact, for example, pushing, grabbing a body part (get your mind out of the gutter, think about grabbing a person's hand to prevent them from taking something off your desk or putting your hands on his or her arm to forcefully turn them to face you), slapping someone (even on the hand), or other seemingly harmless acts of minor violence.

- **Threats of violence.** All threats of violence—even those seemingly made in jest—should be treated with the utmost seriousness. Often threats made in innocuous tones can escalate into actual threats, the example I provided earlier about the man who would say, "someday I'm going to come in and kill all of you" should not have been ignored. But this was before the rash of workplace gun violence and I was young and stupid.
- **Jokes about violence.** I worked in an organization where merely joking about violence was grounds for dismissal. This place took the policy to such an extreme that we couldn't even use the term "bullet points" because "bullet is a violent word". I argued (in vain) that the origin of the word "bullet" came from Roman "bulletin", that is, a list of bullets read in public as sort of the ancient equivalent of a news broadcast.

I never gave up my fight against what I then saw as stupidity and political correctness, at one point they sent a memo telling each of us that we had to report to HR to get new "headshots" for our ID badges. I incredulously responded, "Oh, we can't say "bullet" but we can say "headshot"!!! I believed that the policy was dim-witted and frankly embarrassing, but in the light of the many single-shooter events, I now realize that words matter. What we say often belies what we think so the no joking about violence is, in my opinion, a good policy, but by now you know I have no use for political correctness (don't get me wrong I am not actively looking to offend people, but people **take** offense when others aren't deliberately **giving** it) and I still say bullet points with a strange sense of satisfaction.

Dress Codes

A relatively easy precautionary measure for preventing workplace violences are dress codes or uniforms. Dress codes can serve several purposes:

1. **They make outsiders easy to identify.** Whether it be company logo golf shirts, or simply clearly delineated "business casual" setting a strong "look" for your company makes it easy to tell at a glance who belongs in an area and who does not. This not only protects your staff from violent intruders, but also from theft.

    I worked at a company where a team of thieves dressed in suits and ties walked through the company looking for unattended wallets and purses, social security numbers, and whatever things of value they could lay hands on. Their mistake was dressing like Jules and Vincent from *Pulp Fiction* while the rest of us were all in a strictly defined business casual. (Well that and the fact that we were all required to wear name badges in

157

plain sight above the waste at all times AND most everyone at the 800-person facility knew one another, or at least the people who were authorized to be in their work areas.

A comical cat-and-mouse pursuit ensued (after the police were called) as three maintenance men ran through the building looking for the thieves. Their final take was $6 and some change that an accountant had left in his jacket pocket (and I'm still not convinced that he didn't make that up for attention.)

2. **They discourage gang activity.** Many of the places I have worked specifically forbade gang colors and in areas where gangs were prevalent workers were issued uniforms. This may seem like overkill (see I still use words that denote violence, I can't help it, there are too many idioms embedded in our lexicon) but taking such measures can literally mean the difference between life and death. If there isn't a gang presence you probably don't have to take such extreme measures, but where there is a gang presence—even a small one—you must make every effort to keep gang members from your workplace.

3. **Dress codes make it easier to spot changes in hygiene and grooming.** The point of a dress code is to ensure that everyone looks enough alike that they are easily identifiable as an employee, but there is an additional advantage. When a worker is out of dress code, suddenly wears soiled, foul-smelling, or unkempt clothing to work, it can be an indicator of trouble outside of work that could make the worker a candidate for performing a violent act, or a potential target.

At a minimum dress codes should include an identification badge with the photo of the employee. This badge should be worn above the waste at all times while an individual is on the premises. Ideally, the badge will double as a key card.

Communication Policies

Notification of Employment Termination

Perhaps the most overlooked and dangerous omissions is the announcement of an employee's departure from the company. This is another area where, if you're not careful, you could needlessly find yourself in legal hot water. Many organizations, afraid that if they describe the circumstances of a worker's departure might get sued. Yet your workforce needs to be aware of the people who are no longer employees. This doesn't just apply to people who have been fired or quit on very bad terms. Even employees who leave the company on the very best terms present a risk, albeit a very low one, and your staff has a right to know who is a worker and who is not. You may indeed get sued for disclosing confidential information, but you needn't disclose confidential information.

The following two email communications say essentially the same thing:

> Sally Murdoch has decided to pursue other career opportunities and as of December 1st she will no longer

be employed here at Peaceco. We wish Sally every success in her future endeavors.

And,

Effective December 1st Sally Murdoch is no longer employed here at Peaceco.

Which of these two indicate that Sally might be a threat risk? Neither? Both? It doesn't really matter, what matters the most in this situation is that everyone knows that Sally is no longer an employee and that she—no matter what the circumstances of her departure—needs to be treated in the same way as any other non-employee. What's the difference between an ex-employee and a non-employee? Nothing. In our example, people need to understand that Sally Murdoch—whether loved or despised—must be treated in the same way as any other visitor to the facility and there can be NO EXCEPTIONS!

Neither of these statements discloses confidential information. Keep your communications informative enough to provide the necessary information (what date is the separation is effective, and of course who is leaving) but you needn't any other details. If someone wants to know where Sally is going, they can ask Sally—don't share the name of her new employer with the company; she may have decided to leave to escape an aggressive coworker.

Weapons Policy

The best practice in weapons policy is to have no weapons allowed on the premises[25], including any company property or event (this would include the parking lot or the company picnics). Here again the law is a bit murky. Do you have a right to search an employee's personal car? That depends on your State Law (here again consult your legal counsel, seriously, for what you're paying your lawyers they had ought to be made to earn it). In general, you have the right (see my previous statement) to search a car if it is a company car or a rental car for which has been paid by the company, but employees still have their fourth amendment rights against unreasonable search and seizure. Even in States that have "open carry" laws there are limitations as to where weapons are not allowed, and many States have upheld a business's right to further curtail these rights.

Some will argue that armed workers are better able to protect themselves in single-shooter events, but when the police arrive, they are not likely to suss out the good guys from the bad guys when people are being shot. Law officers will, and should, shoot armed civilians first and ask questions later. I could agree with proponents of arming the workforce but then we would all be wrong. Do we really want our workplaces to become old west saloons where Bill guns down Nancy for drinking the last of the coffee and failing to make a fresh pot? I for one do not, and I don't even drink coffee!

---

[25] *This statement is in no way the universal opinion of experts in violence prevention, and many of you are likely turned off by this statement. In preparation for this this book I interviewed several very helpful law enforcement personnel and there was no consensus. What was clear, however, is that those in favor of arming your workplace put so many qualifiers on their assertion that employees should be armed—if the employee is highly trained, and if the employee is comfortable with guns, if the the employee is capable of taking a human life, if the employee does not use drugs or alcohol, that I made a command decision and sided with those who opposed arming their employees. That having been said, all I spoke to agreed that it is far more effective to identify and protect potential targets and to identify and avoid hiring potential threats.*

Chapter 8: Workplace security

When we think about workplace security, too many organizations focus on keeping people from stealing, misusing their computer to visit pornagraphic websites, or other nonsense that makes people think that the company thinks that they are liars, cheats, and thieves. We have got to abandon this kind of thinking and focus on keeping weapons and rampaging maniacs out of the workplace, and that begins by turning your workplace from a "soft target" to a "hard target".

Mass Shootings versus Workplace Violence

Mass shootings and workplace violence overlap. The teacher shot dead during a mass shooting is different from a teacher shot dead by her estranged husband while she is at work. While both are tragic, the motivation of the shooter is usually quite different. Since the motivation is different so to must be the response.

One thing that both have in common is the preference for "soft targets" over "hard targets". The shooters typically are either looking for either a large body count in the case of a mass shooting or to kill a specific person or people. Either way the perpetrator usually takes the path of least resistance.

So why attack someone at the workplace? Simple, because it's relatively easy—-if you are an estranged domestic partner your target may be in hiding, have a protective order that neighbors know about, or have other people armed and waiting. The one fairly immalleable variable that makes the target vulnerable is work. The target may have overlooked this variable or be leery (either out of embarrassment or for fear of negative job ramifications) of informing his or her employer of the situation.

Make Your Facility A "Hard Target"

Mass killers like "soft targets"—places like schools, movie theaters, and according to the US Department of Homeland Security's website, "Soft Targets and Crowded Places (ST-CPs), such as sports venues, shopping venues, schools, and transportation systems, are locations that are easily accessible to large numbers of people and that have limited security or protective measures in place making them vulnerable to attack. DHS has been working for many years to address ST-CP security and preparedness, with recent shifts in the threat landscape calling for renewed departmental focus on leveraging and maximizing its ST-CP security authorities, capabilities, and resources in an integrated and coordinated manner.[26] They like soft targets because people tend to be easily accessible making it easy to quickly kill many people without a whole lot of effort. So your first order of business should be to transform your soft target environment into a hard target environment.

_____

[26]*Source: https://www.dhs.gov/publication/securing-soft-targets-and-crowded-places*

Most workplaces are unwittingly soft targets and one of the first steps you can do reduce your risk is to close the gaping holes in your facility's security. As a consultant, I visit hundreds of workplaces and it's amazing to me how lax some companies' security is.

Let me illustrate two different approaches. In one company I visited often years ago, my car was stopped at the gate where an armed security guard, checked the visitor's list. If, as was often the case, my client had forgotten to put me on the visitor's list, I was instructed to back up and park about 20 yards from the guard shack (I wasn't allowed to even enter the grounds to turn my vehicle around). I would have to wait patiently until my contact came and collected me.

After a stern talking to about protocols the guard would put my name on the visitor's list and I was allowed to (after receiving a parking pass, park in the assigned visitor parking. Before I could proceed, I was told by the officer that even if I had an open carry weapons permit no weapons were allowed on the premises and that the premises included the parking lot. I was further told that in entering the parking lot I was voluntarily agreeing to having my car and belongings searched for cause or for no cause.

Once parked, my contact would escort me to the lobby, where I was again required to show government issued identification and the receptionist would create a temporary visitor's badge for me. My contact was required to escort me everywhere I went, and all the doors had keycard access (including the restrooms). Fortunately, my escort wasn't required to monitor my excretory activities, but he was required to wait outside until I finished.

All the production area doors were key coded including the roller doors that vehicles travelled in and out of the production area. Truck drivers were confined to a small office where they too were under the vigilant eye of another armed security guard. It should be noted that this facility did not manufacture weapons or top-secret items nor had they ever had a workplace violence incident. It all seemed like a bit much, but nobody was ever murdered there. It was a "hard target"

At the other extreme was a company that had no guarded main gate and there were so many unlocked doors that not only COULD I bypass the reception, I often (at the urging and encouragement of my client) DID bypass the reception. The reception area was the only area of monitored ingress, and were I a mad dog killer one bullet would have taken her out and granted me access to the entire facility.

The similarities of the cultures of these two organizations were virtually identical, and as we have discussed prior to this, no company is immune to a single shooter event. But the first company took the possibility of a violent intruder extremely seriously, and I never once felt inconvenienced or upset.

Turning your organization into a hard target is not as difficult as you might imagine. First there should be multiple checkpoints before entering the main facility. The first should be a guard shack where all visitors must check in. Employees should be issued photo ID badges programmed to allow them to unlock only the doors to which they have access.

Next, visitors should be escorted from the guard shack to the main reception area where their names and company are recorded in the visitor badge. The best practice in company security is to only admit visitors who have a photo identification and are then issued a visitor badge with their photos on the badge (there are many inexpensive systems that will allow badge creation, don't freak out that this is going to cost so much your company won't go for it or your company is too small to do all this.) Your key card system should be capable of having central points of control that can lockdown the system in case of an intrusion.

Although the hip new thing in office layout is the "Open Space" work environment—and having worked in one I found it to be a very pleasant work surrounding, but, unless very specific security measures are taken these layouts can create a soft target environment. It may run counter-intuitive but even these open areas can be made more secure.

For starters, the kind of rigor shown in my first example at the beginning of this chapter. The entrance to these areas (including the requirement to use a key card to go to a specific elevator floor) should be tightly controlled. In any workplace, employers should take pains to ensure that nobody can travel to areas where they don't have a legitimate business purpose. And while an open floor plan allows a single shooter to the opportunity to kill multiple victims even these areas can be key carded and made very difficult to move quickly from area to area. Additionally, most of these areas have "privacy rooms" (I will spare you the tasteless and off-color names I had for these rooms) that are small rooms with no windows.

The doors to these rooms should have locks on them and people should be instructed to go to these rooms and lock the door during an emergency. It is important that each person is assigned a room where they should go BEFORE an actual event because an innovative gunman could put a gun to someone's head and force the people inside to open it with the threat of harming the individual. Also, by having assigned rooms, the people inside know who they can safely let into the locked room and who they should not. It's cold hearted I know, but better that one person dies than 10.

Another way to protect yourself from a single-shooter who is trying to gain access to the premises by forcing a hostage to "escort" him through the key carded areas, is the use of duress code words. These code words alert the security guards or other gatekeeper that you are being forced to escort someone against your will. The word should be common enough so that a person in a highly stressful situation can easily work them into a conversation but not so common that a person might inadvertently trigger an alarm. For example, a duress word might be "strawberry" and the person being held hostage could alert the guard by politely asking the security guard if his wife Susan is still selling strawberry jelly, this becomes especially powerful if the security guard is unmarried, or his wife is named anything but Susan. The security guard should have the hostage sign in as a visitor and once the two have passed the gates, sound the alarm and lock down the facility.

Once locked down the security guard (or receptionist if a security guard isn't the gatekeeper) should immediately dial 911 and follow the procedures of his/her department (these will differ from company to company and are far too diverse to list here). Duress-codes should be changed frequently and not have the obvious flaw of being known to recently dismissed employees.

Chapter 9: Surviving a Single Shooter Event

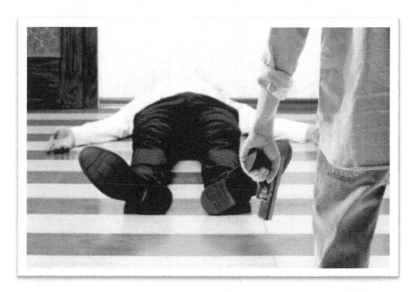

Whether or not your employees survive a single shooter event relies to a great extent on their ability to act quickly and without thinking. In the research of this book I found that most sources I found offered tips for protecting yourself were for random single shooter events on soft targets. My advice is re-read Chapter 7 and make darned sure that your workplace is not a soft target. That having been said, the time to think about surviving a single shooter event is long before the event occurs. You and all your employees, visitors, and vendors should know precisely what to do before an event occurs.

Training

The best policies in the world are useless if no one knows them. Additionally, compliance with the policies will greatly increase if you the people understand WHY the policy exists. Violence prevention training should outline each policy, explain its intent and purpose, and talk about the disciplinary consequences for not following procedures. You should also reinforce the evacuation procedures, when and where to hide if you are in the immediate vicinity of the shooter, and how to know when it is safe to come out of hiding.

Training should not be a singular event given to workers during an orientation where you cram as much information into their dazed skulls as you can in the shortest amount of time. Instead, use safety talks, news reports of mass shootings, and safety moments at meetings to reinforce the topic of exactly what the policies and procedures are for preventing and surviving the unlikely event of a workplace violence incident.

You should also engage in a rigorous program of refresher training to ensure that people know by rote every policy and procedure related to workplace violence. This may seem a bit much, but training people about your attendance policy is far less important than keeping people alive.

Drills

Most of us can remember the fire drills of their school days. I can remember mine particularly acutely because my principle had been a teacher who survived a school fire in which several faculty and around 30[27] students died horribly in the fire. She was obsessed with fire safety and I could probably have gotten away with blasphemy (it was Catholic School) before I would be forgiven for horsing around during a fire drill. And these were no ordinary drills either. She would time us and lecture us or commend us depending on our evacuation time.

She would throw us curve balls like blocking one or more of the doors with barricades to simulate an evacuation route blocked by fire. All of it seemed pointless, silly and ridiculous to my fourth-grade mind, but I can tell you this, I can get out of a burning school building in less than 2 minutes 30 seconds to this day without panicking! And THAT is what you want to achieve with gun violence drills—you want to automate

---

[27] *To the best of my recollection, my late mother told me the story and I'm not sure if I'm remembering all the details correctly but the point remains valid.*

people's responses so that they don't have to think about where they will walk rapidly[28] and hide.

Frequent drills are so effective that your workforce is likely to be able to automatically react to a workplace violence without hesitation, gaining valuable seconds that can save lives.

During the Event

During a incident of workplace violence every second counts and a moment lost can mean the difference between life and death. There are small but important differences between reacting to a random mass shooting and an incident of workplace violence. Survival in an incident of workplace violence may well depend on how quickly and efficiently you execute these steps:

1. **Sound the alarm.** As soon as you suspect that an incident of workplace violence is, or about to be, underway call security of 911. Quickly report the presence of an armed intruder and your location. If at any point you feel that you are in imminent danger, slowly put the phone down leaving it off the hook. This way emergency responders are can hear what's going on and, in some cases, have a better chance of quickly reaching the location.

---

[28] *There are experts in single shooter events that will recite the mantra "Run, Hide, and Fight" which is good advice in a soft target random violence situation, but I disagree with it in a workplace setting. Humans are predators with eyes adapted to cue in on movement. Moving rapidly but not running lessens the chance that you will trip, is less likely to draw the attention of the shooter, and allows reduces the chance that you will panic.*

2. **Take cover.** Follow the fire drill rules here. Stop work, turn off your phone, and silently walk—not run[29] [30]—to the nearest room that has no windows and a door that can be locked. Watch for other employees headed your way and continue to quickly get as many coworkers into the room before closing and locking it. Once the door is closed and locked do not reopen it until an all clear signal has sounded. Turn off the light if you are able to do so. If you get to the room once it has been locked move to your secondary hiding spot. Do not panic, scream, cry, or pound on the door. Move stealthily to a spot that is outside the line of vision ideally behind shelves, file cabinet or something else that is durable enough to lessen a bullet penetrating it.

   Telling you to stay calm is like you telling me to be taller, BUT as much as possible, stay in control of yourself and the situation. Workplace shooters tend to enjoy and feed on chaos, an apparently empty work area isn't an attractive hunting ground for a mass shooter and he is more likely to move on than to waste precious seconds playing hide and seek. Time is the enemy of a lone gunman

3. **Fight back, but only as a last resort.** It's easy to say, "I'm not going to sit there and wait to be killed" but that's exactly what a lot of people do. Remember, he may have a gun but you have home field advantage. Workplace shootings typically are over long before the police arrive, so the shooters tend to strike quickly and either flee or kill themselves very quickly. It may seem

---

[29] *Here again this is a hotly contested assertion. One school of thought (from those who have has apparently never hunted deer or any other animal capable of running) argues that it is "almost impossible" to hit a running target. The trophy head on my brother-in-law's wall would argue that point if it could. As a general rule if you have not been spotted by the shooter rapidly exit the area, but if the gun is pointed at you, run like a spotted-ass ape.*

[30] *Remember, movement, especially sudden movement attracts the attention of predators*

4. like hours, but the average event is typically measured in minutes. Before fleeing to your hiding spot grab your scissors or any of a dozen office supplies that can be used as a weapon. If you are discovered by the gunman don't try to bargain with him, instead use the scissors to stab him in the eye, ribcage, or underarm. You may lose that fight, but you will cost the shooter time that he can't afford to lose. Remember this is the last resort so don't try to be a hero and don't go on the offensive unless you have truly no other choice.

Dealing with police/first responders

If you were able to get out of the kill zone, you may have to help the first responders by telling them:

- Is the shooter still on the premises?
- Who is the shooter?
- What does the shooter look like?
- With what is the shooter armed?[30]
- When did the event start?
- Who is the target?
- Where on the premises is the shooter (if you know) or where are the victims?
- Approximately how many victims are there?

You will be likely in shock or another highly emotional state. Your coworkers and friends need you to stay calm and as lucid as you can be. Practice talking to first responders during drills and gather as much information as you possibly can while you wait for the first responders.

---

[30] *You need not be an expert in weaponry to distinguish between a gun and a knife, a pistol and a rifle, or an automatic pistol and a revolver.*

Chapter 10: Crisis Management: Dealing with the Aftermath

Y ou won't feel like it, but as soon as the event is over, write down or record as many details as you can recall. A crime has been committed and if the shooter survives, he will likely to be criminally prosecutors and your notes about the attack could be vital in his prosecution. If the perpetrator escapes, your notes, including a physical description and what he was wearing also can be especially helpful. Do not return to your work area until the police have finished processing the scene.

Dealing with traumatized employees and families

The true aftermath can be a lengthy process, and it will take a long time before the survivors will feel safe again. Hiring professional grief counselors can help survivors to work through their difficult emotions and expedite the process of returning to something approaching normal, and you should offer this service to the families of the victims. Some survivors may develop Post Traumatic Stress Disorder (PTSD) a serious mental condition that may mean that they may not be able to return to the scene of the crime for many months, if ever.

I worked at one company who brought in grief counselors after the unexpected heart attack death of an employee. These people looked like the dregs scooped out of the septic tank of a failed hippie commune and were just plain ODD. No one, and I mean NOT A SINGLE PERSON availed themselves of their services. Buy me a beer and I will tell you the whole sordid tale of what happens when you make an unqualified imbecile the head of Human Resources. But just because this company overreacted and hired a really poor cultural fit in its choice of grief counsellors doesn't mean that grief counselors are a bad idea. Here is a couple of ways the bungling vice president screwed up (and how you can prevent your company from doing so):

- **Panic buying**. A good Human Resources department, and fairly or unfairly in a lot of companies this is considered an oxymoron, will already have identified a source of grief counsellors who specialize in recovering from a workplace homicide.
- **Provide privacy.** In the case of the company to which I am referring the grief counselors were put in offices with windows so anybody who happened by could see who was seeking help. The identities of those who chose to seek help should be protected.
- **Recognize that grieving is a process.** Grief is a process, and it is often delayed. Some people grief immediately but most begin the process by struggling to process and make sense of what happened. The grieving process can take months or longer.
- **Some people will require more than grief counselling.** Often, survivors of a workplace homicide will develop Post Traumatic Stress Disorder (PTSD) and my require a lifetime of treatment for this. You should identify treatment resources and options NOW.

Dealing with the media

Workplace violence is news and the kind of news that it often reported live. After you have dealt with the actual violent encounter, your first responsibility is to the victims and you must never lose sight of that. Ideally, the news media would leave you alone long enough to gather the facts before bombarding you with questions, but in today's 24-hour news cycle that is not often common practice; the reality is the media needs the quick story. While situations like this it may be unpalatable to some, the press has an important job to do, and workplace violence is big news.

You need to develop (or if you already have developed, review and if necessary, revise) a crisis management plan. The plan should include sections on other events but **must** include a section on who is authorized to be a spokesperson for the company. This isn't just about protecting the company, but also about protecting the workers, and not violating privacy or other laws.

Reporters and news crew may actually arrive before the police or rescue vehicles. Controlling the message, you want to send is crucial and one wrong word can turn you from a sympathetic victim to a callous corporate jerk. As with everything else, a successful reaction to the the event begins by preparing for the event long before the it occurs.

When I say "control the message" I am not encouraging you to lie or mislead the media. Years ago, I worked for a small-town paper as a community stringer—I went to city council meetings and listened to small town whiners complain to small town idiots who ran for office simply to feel important and so that they could go to meetings. I was paid a walloping $6 a story but eventually was writing so much (including a humor article, where I learned that no matter WHAT you say, you WILL offend somebody. It was a good experience because I stopped caring about how people would react to my writing and more about the substance of my writing) that while never officially made a full reporter, I was soon making a lot more than the staff reporter who complained bitterly. I could write fast and I could get local politicians to go on the record with comments. Why? Because the liked and trusted me. The staff reporter didn't have that same rapport, this was his *career* whereas for me it was the third of the three jobs I was working and was essentially just beer money. The staff reporter was a good guy (although a little self-important for a 22-year old reporter for a paper with a circulation of around 16) but in his drive to get an accurate and interesting story he would often anger the local politicians by reporting exactly what they said, usually something stupid and emotional. The politicians would cry foul and demand a retraction or an apology, which the editor refused to do on an accurate story. So, the politicians refused to talk to the staff reporter and requested me instead. This wasn't the case with EVERY politician, but enough to really ire the staff reporter.

I was different. I didn't expect a Pulitzer prize for the articles I wrote and I (this will shock you) took a far more moderate approach. I wanted the truth, but I also knew that sometimes people say things in the heat of the moment that aren't fit for print. In one case I was covering a story where the Mayor erupted into a heated argument with a councilman when I asked the Mayor for comment, he said, "that guy is just an asshole". I asked him if he was SURE he wanted to say that, and to my surprise, he angrily said, "YES!"

I could have run the comment replacing the insult with the common newspaper "(expletive)" I took another tact. I waited a day and called the Mayor again. He greeted me cordially, and I asked him quite frankly what spin did he want to put on this story. Did he want to seem like a foul-mouthed aggressor or someone who was provoked to the point where any reasonable man would lose his temper? He thought about it and decided that the message he wanted to send was that he was never going to back down to someone when such an important issue was at stake. I don't remember his exact quote, but it was something like a City Councilman couldn't just get his way by provoking a shouting match and expected more professionalism in the future, but whatever the case, the decisions before the Council would not be decided by he who yells the loudest. The mayor loved the story.

Part of my secret to my success was that I took the time to get to know the Mayors and the members of the City Council and as a result, I never had a single claim that I had misquoted someone or had taken something they said out of context.

One tip I used to give when I taught executives crisis management was to buy a reporter lunch. By getting to know your local news media personally, it makes your job of being a spokesperson during a crisis much easier. It is tough to portray someone you know as a heartless corporate puke bag if you know them, especially if you have broken bread together. That doesn't mean that the reporter will go easy on you if you are genuinely in the wrong, but it does mean that more often than not they will give you a fair shot and be more impartial in difficult times. Plus, reporters don't make a lot of money and appreciate a free meal; I know I did.

The spokesperson needs to control the message from the very first minute the crisis unfolds. The message should contain four major elements:

1. What happened? Don't speculate, rather tell the reporters the facts as you know them so far.

2. How do you feel about this? Obviously, you should start about how you empathize with the victims and their families, but you should also express what you are feeling? Do you feel angry because an attack on any of your employees feels like an attack on you? (if you do feel angry be sure you never inadvertently direct that anger at anyone except the perpetrator) Are you sad because you knew some of the victims? Don't be afraid to be human or to express your emotions—if the reporters don't get it from you, they will seek out grieving employees or families.

3. Facts about your company or gun violence—remember reporters likely know nothing or very little about the subject and you have a unique opportunity to educate them; don't force them to fill in the blanks.

4. What you intend to do. Be careful with this one, because you don't really have enough facts yet to know where there were security breaches or system flaws that created the environment that precipitated the violence. But you can say something like, "we intend to find out how this was possible and take every measure necessary to ensure that our people are, and feel, safe while working here.

Provide early information to the press while acknowledging that you do not have all the facts. Don't be afraid to say that you don't know; just make sure to communicate what you DO know. Stay on message! Make sure that you train the spokesperson to truly be a mediator between what is happening inside of the organization and relay that accurately to the outside world—that is, the media and the community.

Have trusted members of your crisis management team speak with as many employees as possible to gain insights into the organization's state of minds and report it back to the company spokesperson. Adjust the message as needed to accurately reflect what is going on at the current time. It is important to never lose sight of what is important in the midst of tragedy: showing the compassion you feel for your people and expressing sympathy for the individuals and their families affected by the tragedy.

Accurate reporting by the media can be very useful in keeping concerned family members and curious bystanders away because the bulk of the people watching will prefer to satisfy their curiosity from the safety of their own homes than watching from a vantage point that could get them killed.

Tell the media what as soon as you can the details that you know for a fact. Explain the steps you are taking to ensure—as much as possible—that such an event does not happen at your organization and what you intend to do to remedy and of the issues that made this event possible. Lastly, tell the media when they can expect to hear from you again. Also establish and maintain lines of open and honest communication.

Chapter 11: What Can I Do?

There is a lot of grim material in this book, but take heart there's still hope. Your creepy coworker probably won't go on a killing spree, and you ex probably won't try to kill you. The best news though is there are things you can do to protect yourself and your coworkers:

1. Forewarned is forearmed. Now that you have read this take the time to look around your workplace and:
   a. Determine your escape route.
   b. Determine an alternative escape route.
   c. Preprogram the numbers for internal security, 911(including the numbers required to access an outside line), and Human Resources into your desk or cell phone.
   d. Identify the closest secure hiding place.

e. Identify a makeshift weapon like a pair of scissors or a heavy lamp that you can easily take with you as you evacuate.

2. Familiarize yourself with your company's policies regarding workplace violence.

3. Remind coworkers to obey the rules designed to protect you.

4. If you see something suspicious in the behavior ask them if everything is okay. They might tell you to mind your own business. IT IS YOUR BUSINESS!!

5. Intervene early.

6. Alert Human Resources of erratic behavior of coworkers.

7. Flee dangerous situations early; better safe than sorry and better safe than dead.

8. Don't panic. You got this.

Conclusion

Years ago when my daughter was about four years old we were watching television together and in the course of the fictitious drama there was a murder. Nothing graphic or even remarkable. She recoiled in shock and horror. I explained to her that most people don't get murdered and in fact most people won't even KNOW anyone who will get murdered.

She looked at me quizzically and asked that if that was the case why was it always on TV. I explained that the programs on TV were entertainment and people were entertained by things outside their personal experience.

Years later we were watching an episode of the show Friends I told my now 10-year old daughter that not everyone in their twenties were hopping in and out of bed with everyone they just met.

She nonchalantly said, "I know dad, it's like the murder". I was baffled. I asked her what she meant and she reminded me, and with much effort of our conversation so many years before, she finished by saying it was entertainment and not real life.

Unfortunately life is imitating art and we now life in a world where if we are going to take active steps to protect ourselves.

Remember, workplace the incidents of workplace violence are happening more frequently and in the current societal climate of hate and intolerance, no workplace is immune from a single shooter workplace event.

That doesn't mean we are powerless, however, by working with your executive team to create a crisis management plan, with first responders, and by drilling and training your workforce you can often reduce the carnage a lone gunman can create.

We may never completely eliminate workplace violence, but one thing is clear: as long as pundits keep telling people to respond to workplace violence in the same way as they respond to mass shootings the carnage will continue.

When it comes to workplace violence the rule isn't:

1. Run

2. Hide

3. Fight back,

rather the rule is

1. Predict

2. Prevent

3. Restrict

4. Restrain

5. Turn it over to law enforcement

About the Author

Phil La Duke is the author of the popular book on workplace safety, I *Know My Shoes Are Untied. Mind Your Own Business.* A self-described provocateur La Duke has poked and prodded the world of worker safety for over a decade. In this work, La Duke takes on an issue that is personal to him: workplace violence (no he didn't shoot up his workplace.) He has worked at and with companies that have experienced workplace violence. His work will advise you, provoke you, inform you, and infuriate you, but when the dust settles the points he makes, and practical tips he offers will stay with you and gnaw at you like a rat until you finally act and make your workplace a safer and more secure place of employment.

33938112R00106

Made in the USA
Middletown, DE
20 January 2019